Selection Theory and Social Construction

SUNY series in Philosophy and Biology
David Edward Shaner, Editor

Selection Theory and Social Construction

The Evolutionary Naturalistic Epistemology of Donald T. Campbell

EDITED BY

Cecilia Heyes and David L. Hull

State University of New York Press

Published by
State University of New York Press, Albany

Printed in the United States of America

For information, address State University of New York Press,
90 State Street, Suite 700, Albany, NY 12207

Production by Diane Ganeles
Marketing by Anne M. Valentine

Library of Congress Cataloging-in-Publication Data

Selection theory and social construction : the evolutionary naturalistic epistemology of Donald T. Campbell / edited by Cecilia Heyes and David L. Hull.
p. cm. — (SUNY series in philosophy and biology)
Includes bibliographical references and index.
ISBN 0-7914-5055-4 (alk. paper) — ISBN 0-7914-5056-2 (pbk. : alk. paper)
1. Social sciences—Research—Methodology. 2. Knowledge, Theory of. 3. Campbell, Donald Thomas, 1916–1997. I. Heyes, Cecilia M. II. Hull, David L. III. Series.

H62 .S4172 2001
300'.72—dc21

00-051019

10 9 8 7 6 5 4 3 2 1

Contents

Donald T. Campbell. Photo courtesy of Barbara Frankel and Syracuse University.

1

Introduction

CECILIA HEYES

The breadth of Donald Campbell's scholarship was such that he made significant, enduring contributions to social psychology, anthropology, sociology, education, science studies and epistemology. A previous volume in his honor (Brewer and Collins, 1981) provided an admirable representation of this breadth, with chapters sampling many aspects of Campbell's research, from the technicalities of program evaluation to the abstractions of hypothetical realism. The present volume, in contrast, focuses on Campbell's studies of knowledge; on his elaboration of the evolutionary naturalistic epistemology which he ultimately preferred to call "selection theory" (Campbell, 1997).

Although he had been publishing on epistemologically relevant topics since the 1950s, in 1986 when I first met Campbell, he continued to see himself as a "pushy outsider" in relation to the community of epistemologists and philosophers of science. This collection of essays does not contradict that typically mocking and astute self-description, but it confirms that the outsider got a long way in; that his central epistemological claims were heard, and that they have effected change and excited controversy that will continue to influence debate in the philosophy and sociology of science for generations.

This introduction has three purposes: to provide a brief biography of Donald Campbell, sketching the roots of his epistemological interests, and including references to his work in this field; to locate Campbell's selection theory in relation to traditional epistemological concerns and social constructivism; and to give an overview of the chapters in this volume.

Biography

Donald T. Campbell (DTC) was born in 1916 in Grass Lake, Michigan, to parents whom he often described as being ready to converse with their children and to answer sensible questions. His grandfather, uncle, and cousins were members of Appalachian Bible-belt free churches, and although DTC had "By high school or early college . . . drifted away from whatever belief in God [he] had had as a child" (Campbell 1988a, p. 21), he recognized in himself the zeal and persistence of an evangelical itinerant preacher.

DTC had great respect for research communities outside the spotlight of premier academic institutions. In line with this, he identified the start of his scholarly career, not with the beginning of his undergraduate years at Berkeley in 1937, but with his arrival at San Bernardino Valley Junior College in 1935. There he learned evolutionary theory from a squirrel hunter and developed his conception of the "worker scientist"; while at Berkeley, as an undergraduate and graduate student in psychology, he was influenced by Egon Brunswik, Edward Tolman, and Robert Tryon. He was involved in data analysis on Tryon's project examining inheritance of maze-running ability in rats, and attended a small seminar group with Tolman and Brunswik, both behaviorist psychologists with a strong interest in philosophy of science and commitment to logical positivism. In contrast with other behaviorists of his day, Tolman saw learners—rat and human—as meandering explorers hoovering up information about their enclosing maze, only a fraction of which would ultimately be useful. So strong was this image in DTC's mind that fifty years later he would impersonate Tolman's intrepid rat, whiskers aquiver, to impress on me, a new post-doctoral student, the inevitably chanciness and wastefulness of knowledge acquisition.

DTC completed his doctoral dissertation on "The Generality of Social Attitude" in 1947, having interrupted his studies from 1941–46 to serve the U.S. war effort, first as a research assistant with Tryon in Washington, and subsequently commanding a naval gun crew on merchant ships sailing between the U.S. and England. In the former role he was exposed to German, Russian, and Italian home propaganda, providing an object lesson in cultural relativism. Having read social science discussions of Nazi ideology and Hitler's *Mein Kampf*, he expected Germany's internal presentation to emphasize the rights of the strong, but found that, like the home propaganda of the Allied nations, it presented the war as essential for defense. DTC said that during his time as a naval officer he "allowed professional content to drop out of [his] life altogether" (Campbell 1988a, p. 5), but that didn't stop him from using a 24-hour leave in 1944 to make a pilgrimage from Liverpool, where his ship was docked, to Cambridge to meet F. C. Bartlett, who was famous for his views on the dynamic, selective character of memory. DTC had traveled for 22 of the 24 hours and, unknown and unexpected, got a cool welcome from Bartlett, but he did not report the episode with any sense of folly. It implies that he was hungry for scholarly contact, and, like the Tolman link, that he was already drawn to selectionist models of knowledge in any available form.

During his first faculty appointment, at Ohio State University (1947–50), DTC taught social psychology, did research on opinion-polling and leadership, and developed his epistemological interests by joining a philosophy of science table each Friday at the faculty club. Kurt Wolff, who was also a regular participant in these discussions, introduced DTC to the sociology of knowledge, and the development of this interest was reflected in his inaugural colloquium, "On the Psychological Study of Knowledge," at the University of Chicago when he became an assistant professor there in 1950. DTC was at the University of Chicago for three years, first as part of the Committee on Education Research and Training in Race Relations, and subsequently in James G. Miller's Committee on Behavioral Sciences. The latter affiliation led him to focus on cybernetics, information theory, and general systems theory, and thereby to examine the relationships between W. Ross Ashby's cybernetics and other natural selection analogues to learning theory and perception. This work appeared a couple of years later in "Adaptive Behavior from Random Response" and "Perception as Substitute Trial and Error" (Campbell 1956a; 1956b), Campbell's first published papers on what he would later describe as "evolutionary epistemology" and, later still, "selection theory."

In 1953, DTC moved from the University of Chicago to Northwestern and remained there for 26 years. Over this period he worked as a social psychologist on social attitude measurement, ethnocentrism, and, most famously, developed techniques of "quasi-experimentation"—research designs and statistical methods enabling rigorous investigation of the effects of manipulated variables under conditions in which random assignment of subjects to groups is impossible. This work made him one of the most frequently cited psychologists in history, and earned him numerous honors, including a Fulbright Professorship at Oxford (1968–69), the American Psychological Society's Distinguished Contribution Award (1970), Presidency of the American Psychological Association (1975), Fellowship of the American Academy of Arts and Sciences (1973), and Membership of the U.S. National Academy of Sciences (1973). Alongside these achievements, however, DTC maintained a strong interest in theory of knowledge, teaching a seminar course on "Knowledge Processes" throughout his time at Northwestern, and regularly publishing essays in which one can trace the development of his selection theory (e.g., Campbell 1956a, 1956b, 1958, 1959, 1960, 1965a, 1966, 1969, 1970, 1973, 1974a, 1974b, 1975b, 1977). High points in this series were the essay "Evolutionary Epistemology," which appeared in a volume honoring Karl Popper (Campbell 1974b), and his William James Lectures, given at Harvard in 1977 and circulated widely in preprint form until their publication eleven years later (Campbell 1988b).

For personal reasons, DTC moved to Syracuse University in 1979, and from there to Lehigh University in 1982, where he remained a University Professor of Social Relations and Psychology until the end of his career. From 1979 onwards, theory of knowledge was his principal focus and the majority of his publications were in this area (e.g., Campbell 1979a, 1979b, 1981b, 1981c, 1982a, 1983a, 1983b, 1984, 1985, 1986a, 1986b, 1987a, 1987b, 1988b, 1988c, 1988d, Campbell & Paller 1989, Campbell 1990a, 1990b, Campbell & Cziko 1990, Campbell 1992, 1993, 1994b). When his final illness began, he was in the middle of assembling an overview of his selection theory, reiterating its principal claims, and indicating those that he would now add or adjust. This final paper was published one year after his death in 1997 (Campbell, 1997).

Epistemology and Social Constructivism

Metaphysics and epistemology are two of the basic areas of philosophy. Metaphysics concerns the fundamental constituents of the world in which we live, while epistemology deals with how we come to know about this world. To a modern reader, metaphysics might sound like physics and epistemology like psychology. The basic constituents of our universe are quarks, prions and the like, while we come to learn about these basic constituents by the methods of science. In the early days of modern philosophy, the ambiguity implicit in the preceding descriptions would have gone unnoticed. Now that science has split off from philosophy, philosophers can be seen to be involved in quite a different activity. Perhaps knowing a good deal of science might help philosophers, but such knowledge is far from sufficient. As far as metaphysics is concerned, philosophers worry about whether a metaphysics of entities and their properties is adequate or whether reference to fields alone will do the trick. Are mental entities part of the furniture of the universe, or can they be explained, possibly explained away, entirely in terms of properties of matter?

Epistemology deals with the justification of whatever beliefs we come to hold. In the early days of modern philosophy, unrealistic standards were assumed in deciding which of our beliefs are justified. Either we know that the earth is roughly spherical in shape with absolute certainty or we know nothing at all. A couple hundred years of philosophical debate resulted in philosophers abandoning such unrealistically high standards for justified knowledge. Another assumption at the time was that the place to begin establishing standards of justified knowledge is the individual human being and his/her interactions with the world in which we live. As it turns out, from this perspective, very little if anything can be known, even on a reasonable notion of justified belief. We do not learn in isolation from all other people. Just as languages are inherently social, so is the acquisition of knowledge. The rallying cry of recent social constructivists is that science is inherently social, and knowledge of social relations is absolutely necessary if we are to understand science. The more ambitious claim of social constructivists is that such social knowledge is also sufficient to explain all the claims made by scientists.

In the past twenty years or so, a variety of novel methods have been used to study science. Scientists deliver papers, discuss their research with each other, publish papers, etc. All of these activities require language. Rhetoricians study the use of language by such language users as politicians and film critics. They have also extended these same modes of explanation to scientists. No one denies that the use of language by scientists has a rhetorical dimension. The issue is whether science is nothing but rhetoric. In the case of all the novel methodologies that are being used to aid in our understanding of science, the conflict arises with respect to the "nothing but" clause preferred by reductionists.

All of us, scientists included, live in a variety of societies and subsocieties. What effects do these societies have on us?

One of the chief occupations of social constructivists is to point out assumptions built into the language that scientists use which seem obviously a feature of their society rather than the particular subject matter of the scientists. For example, evolutionary biologists ask how it is possible for organisms to cooperate in such a competitive process as gene-based biological evolution. They do not ask how it is possible to compete in such a cooperative enterprise. Could it be that we are reading a feature of our societies into the biological world?

Plotkin (this volume) uses the term "social construction" in the context of reductionism. Can descriptive statements made about societies be reduced to psychology or, even more ambitiously, biology? Reductionists claim that in principle, they can, while antireductionists claim that both in practice and in principle they cannot. A $50 note is more than a piece of paper with some printing on it because that is the way that people treat it. In principle, societies are nothing more than people and their interrelations, but the number of people in a society is so large and these interrelations so variable that claims about in-principle reduction may be pie in the sky. In practice, no such reductions can be carried out, nor is there anything gained by ignoring the complex of social relations that characterizes societies. Redescribing a $50 bill in terms of paper and ink accomplishes nothing. However, that Plotkin, a Briton, refers to a $50 "note," while an American refers to the same piece of paper as a $50 "bill," says something about differences in the societies to which the speakers belong.

Total redescription is one thing. Partial redescription is something else. Perhaps not everything about human beings, their psychology and social relations, can be redescribed so that the basic principles of behavioral psychology apply universally, but large segments can be, and these conceptual revisions add to our understanding of the human animal. Picture a behavioral psychologist trying to handle a Freudian dream interpretation. Similar observations hold for the relation between biology and both psychology and sociology. For a very long time both psychologists and sociologists have been aware of what is now termed by evolutionary biologists "parent-offspring conflict." Such conflicts can be explained in part using the techniques of gene-based biological evolution. The point of contention is whether everything about such conflicts can be explained biologically without any reference to the basic principles of psychology and sociology. Conversely, can all of science, including the content of science, be explained totally as nothing but the effects of local, social phenomena? Did Darwin couch his theory in terms of competition among individual organisms because his own Victorian England was so individualistic and competitive? Can the beliefs of social constructivists be explained in the same way?

As Caporael (this volume) points out, Donald Campbell was both a Darwinist and a social constructivist of sorts. In its early versions, evolutionary epistemology was extremely literal. Those organisms that misjudge their environments pay the price of having few, if any, offspring. Some characteristics of organisms, including the human species, can be explained in terms of gene-based biological evolution, but a great deal cannot. Genes have had very little to do with the rise of formal logic in this century, especially since so much of formal logic is so strongly counterintuitive. Perhaps genes provide the necessary prerequisites for coming up with any sort of logic, but that is all. Genes have also had very little to do with the rise in quantum mechanics and relativity theory, both of which are very counterintuitive to ordinary people. As Hull (this volume) argues, Campbell was a "Darwinian" only in the sense that gene-based biological evolution provided one instance of a selection process. He was also a social constructivist in the sense that he thought that the justification of scientific knowledge can be traced to the social organization of science—from evolutionary epistemology via selection theory to a sociology of scientific validity. The status of facts as facts, even social facts, is determined in the context of particular social organizations. Individual scientists are objective in a variety of ways and to various degrees, but the sort of objectivity that counts in science is group objectivity. Because of the social organization of science, scientists are strongly pressured into behaving objectively, like it or not, and enough scientists like it enough of the time for science to have the traditional epistemological characteristics that it is reputed to have.

Overview

Most of the chapters in this volume are concerned with Campbell's claim that all increases in "fit" between systems and their environments arise through the operation of "nested hierarchies" of mechanisms, each operating on the basis of "blind variation and selective retention" (BVSR). The entities involved in variation and selection are themselves various—for example, antibodies in the domain of immunology, hypotheses or ideas in the arena of creative thought, research groups in science, and genes in the seminal case of adaptation through selection—but within each mechanism there is a proliferation of entities, only some of which survive and further proliferate, yielding novelty and increased organization. Campbell's classic statement of this view is his 1974 essay "Evolutionary Epistemology." When we asked each of the contributors to this volume to pick the article by Campbell that had influenced their own work the most directly and substantially, they all cited this paper, a transcript of Campbell's William James Lectures.

In his chapter, Gary Cziko shows how Campbell's BVSR model can be applied to a broad spectrum of cases, from gene-based biological evolution and the reaction of the immune system to antigens, to learning and conceptual change in science. In addition to providing a broad and lucid survey of cases considered by Campbell, he discusses at greater length the operation of BVSR mechanisms in neuroscience, and thereby provides a valuable introduction to a growing field of interest.

In such a broad survey it is possible for Cziko to demonstrate only that, in any given domain and at any given level of organisation, a BVSR mechanism *could* be in operation. It is not possible to consider in detail alternative hypotheses and the kind of evidence that favors, or would favor, the

BVSR option. Campbell's assertion that BVSR is necessary for increases in fit may be taken to mean that there are no such alternatives, but this would be a mistake. His model implies that increases in fit will always be traceable to BVSR in some part of a system, but not that every subcomponent or level of a system will have BVSR characteristics. Thus, the empirical challenge presented by Campbell's selection theory is to identify *where* in any given system BVSR is occuring, to delineate the entities on which it is based, and to model the system-specific mechanisms of proliferation and selective retention.

Cziko also answers some objections to Campbell's evolutionary epistemology raised by Michael Bradie in the chapter that follows. Bradie expands upon his distinction between two programs that are subsumed by evolutionary epistemology: EEM investigates the evolution of epistemic mechanims, and EET the evolution of epistemic theories. In EEM, genetic variation and natural selection are taken literally. Certain ways of perceiving and thinking about the world in which we live are literally programmed into our genes. Bradie sees problems primarily with respect to EET, raising three principal objections. First, he believes that Campbell did not develop one of his central metaphysical concepts, that of "fit" between a system and its environment, in sufficient detail and in a fashion consistent with recent work in evolutionary biology. Second, Bradie claims that Campbell's application of evolutionary epistemology to scientific change is based on a flawed analogy between organism and belief evolution. Organisms, he argues, are selected by "the world in its brute facticity," while in science, beliefs are selected primarily by an environment consisting of other beliefs, data, and explicitly formulated selection criteria. Since by their very nature all analogies are incomplete, we must ask whether the differences between organism and belief evolution *make* a difference. According to Campbell, the principal significance of the *similarites* is that they demonstrate that BVSR is necessary for adaptation and knowledge acquisition, but it is the analytic character of this claim which is the focus of Bradie's third major objection to Campbell's evolutionary epistemology. He argues that if the claim is analytic, then it is untestable, and that untestable claims neither have explanatory power nor a place in descriptive or naturalistic epistemology.

Rather than focusing on the BVSR evolutionary aspect of Campbell's epistemology specifically, two of the contributed chapters, by Ronald Giere and Michael Ruse, proceed from Campbell's commitment to "descriptive" or "naturalistic" epistemology. Believing that this is the only kind of sustainable epistemology, Campbell argued that the search for ultimate justification of knowledge claims must be abandoned, but in favor of "hypothetical realism," not relativism, instrumentalism, or pragmatism. Hypothetical realism posits the existence of an external reality which can be known through perception, learning, and scientific enquiry, but it acknowledges that we can never know with certainty whether specific beliefs arising from these processes are true or justify the global commitment to an external reality. According to Campbell, realism is a hypothesis favored not because it is justified or can provide justification but because it makes sense of, or coheres with, what we (hypothetically) know about evolution, learning and science (Campbell, 1997).

A potential answer to Bradie's third objection, and a great deal more, is provided by Giere in his paper recommending that naturalistic epistemologists take a "methodological turn." In taking such a turn, Campbell's claim that BVSR is necessary for improvements in fit would be recast as a methodological principle characterizing his evolutionary naturalistic epistemology, for example: *For any instance of fit between a system and its environment, seek a BVSR explanation.* Under such a formulation, the principle does not seem to require the kind of transcendental justification that is fundamentally incompatible with naturalism, nor, apparently, does it need to be testable. It could contribute to the production of scientific explanations by promoting the development of specific BVSR hypotheses—hypotheses about the identity of variant generating and selection mechanisms in a given natural domain—which are testable in that domain.

Campbell might have embraced this reformulation of his BVSR claim, and as an avid supporter of maps over words as metaphors for knowledge he would almost certainly have shown enthusiasm for Giere's "perspectival realism," a subtle thesis emphasizing the partiality (incompleteness and interest-relevant character) of scientific knowledge. However, it sometimes seems that Giere is content to eschew ontological questions where Campbell insisted that they be raised. For example, Giere argues that we can use the concept of "fit" between a scientific model and the world without asking whether the model is true, in the correspondence sense, or whether it refers. Campbell, on the other hand, repeatedly insisted that correspondence truth and valid reference should be the explicit goals of science, alongside humble acceptance that whether or not these goals have been achieved can never itself be known.

In contrast with Giere, and in common with Bradie, Ruse takes testability to be the hallmark of naturalistic epistemology. He elaborates five hypotheses about the role of external cultural values in science, and, focusing on biologists' beliefs about progress, attempts to test them against a 200-year historical record of the development of evolutionary theory. After delineating the alternative hypotheses and taking the reader on a fascinating, lightning tour of the relevant history, Ruse concludes that theory development is accompanied by an increase in the influence of internal, epistemic values at the cost of external cultural values, and that the pressure for this transformation comes from scientists' efforts to attain professional status. This conclusion concedes a good deal of ground to the social constructivist portrayal of scientific change while holding fast to substantial remnants of a more traditional, philosophical view, and thus represents a blend of these perspectives very similar to that which Campbell favored.

Kyung-Man Kim addresses the character of variation in BVSR, and in the process responds both to Ruse's early criticisms of the BVSR model of scientific problem solving and some of Bradie's concerns about the "organism and belief evolution analogy." The debate centers on two questions: 1) What did Campbell mean when he claimed that variant generation in science, as in all other domains, is "blind"? 2) What is the significance of the fact that scientists *try* to produce successful hypotheses; that they are intentional problem solvers? Kim argues that Ruse's objections to the application of the BVSR model to science are based on misinterpretation of "blind" to mean "random," and on the insupportable assumption that intentional problem-solving involves some kind of prescience. In this context, it is interesting to note that towards the end of his chapter on progress in evolutionary theory, Ruse emphasizes that contemporary evolutionists actively seek to suppress the influence of external cultural values on their theorizing, and apparently takes this effort as evidence that they succeed.

While Kim defends Campbell's BVSR model of science, Caporael challenges and extends it. Through a close reading of Campbell's work, Caporael first provides a vivid image of the tension that he believed to exist between human social dynamics based on genetic evolution, and the culturally evolved goal of objectivity in science. She portrays Campbell as having seen the (hypothetical) success of science as something which occurs in spite of human sociality, and seeks to replace this view with one that escapes gene-culture duality, emphasizes the similarity between the social dynamics of science and of hunter-gatherer societies, and casts these dynamics as more naturally cooperative than Campbell and other evolutionists are typically willing to accept.

A key component of Caporael's model of the evolution of sociality is the claim that "core configurations," types of social groups, are repeatedly assembled in cultural evolutionary time. The term "repeated assembly" indicates that formation of these groups, rather than being genetically determined, is influenced by cognitive abilities that have co-evolved with the configurations themselves, and by consistent environmental demands from the asocial environment. Although Caporael's model contrasts with Campbell's, she makes use of an important Campbellian "tool": the notion of "downward causation" (1974a, 1990, 1994b).

Plotkin also uses the concept of downward causation, but his project is very different from Caporael's. Phillip Kitcher has warned that culture will not come within the explanatory reach of natural science "without a serious psychological theory onto which the considerations about cultural transmission can be grafted." Guided by this challenge, Plotkin tries to identify the kind of psychological theory which could provide a basis for this grafting, and concludes that the best candidate is a nativist, Chomsky-esque theory of language. Thus, in contrast with Caporael, who regards Campbell as having overestimated the role of genetic mechanisms in shaping cultural beliefs and practices, Plotkin emphasizes the degree to which BVSR at the genetic level influences cultural change.

In the final chapter, David Hull looks very carefully at the temporal development of Campbell's naturalistic epistemology. The general view is that Campbell was reasoning by analogy from gene-based selection in biological evolution to other forms of BVSR, but from his earliest writings Campbell was attempting to develop a general analysis of selection that applies equally to all forms of selection. Hull also argues that in Campbell's later years he came to think that the epistemological warrant of science flows not from the involvement of selection *per se* but from its social organization, what Campbell called "the sociology of scientific validity."

Each of the authors of this volume acknowledges the importance of Donald Campbell's contributions to epistemology by criticizing, defending and/or extending them. In addition, and without any prompting from the editors, each contributor chose to pay tribute to Campbell in a personal note at the beginning or the end of his or her chapter. These paragraphs describe the extraordinary warmth, generosity, and playfulness of a great scholar.

2

Universal Selection Theory and the Complementarity of Different Types of Blind Variation and Selective Retention

GARY A. CZIKO

No one had more influence on my career and professional interests than did Don Campbell, even though it was not until I was well into my mid-career years and Campbell was approaching the end of his that I felt his influence.

At the time, I was involved in research on child language development and had been first seduced and then troubled by Chomsky's innatist solution to the puzzle of language acquisition. Then in the summer of 1987 I read *The Blind Watchmaker*, Dawkins's (1986) lively and provocative book on evolution. Having come to appreciate for the first time the formidable power of the process of cumulative variation and selection, I couldn't help wondering if the process was applicable beyond the domain of biological evolution. If cumulative variation and selection operating among organisms could generate all the world's marvelously designed living forms without preordained plans or prior knowledge, then why couldn't such a process occurring *within* the human brain underlie the acquisition of human language without the innate plans and prior knowledge of Chomksy's postulated universal grammar? And why couldn't such a process underlie the emergence of other forms of knowledge as well, such as scientific and technological knowledge?

I mentioned these half-baked ideas to Howard Gruber, a developmental psychologist and Darwin scholar (see his *Darwin on Man*, 1974) who was at the University of Geneva where I was spending my sabbatical leave from the University of Illinois. Gruber responded with something like, "Oh, you must have been reading Don Campbell." Since at the time I knew only of Campbell's work on social science research methodology (e.g., Campbell & Stanley, 1966; Cook & Campbell, 1979), I was puzzled by the reference to Campbell but I did not reveal my ignorance to Gruber.

I didn't get the chance to follow up on his remark until I returned to Illinois in the summer of 1988. Then I discovered Campbell's 1960 *Psychological Review* paper, "Blind Variation and Selective Retention in Creative Thought as in Other Knowledge Processes" and my world changed. Reading this paper I was both thrilled and disappointed to find that Campbell had developed 28 years earlier many of the ideas that were just beginning to form in my mind. I asked my colleague Bob Stake (who always seemed to know anybody worth knowing) if he knew where Campbell could be reached and he provided me with Don's telephone number at Lehigh University in Bethlehem, Pennsylvania.

I called Don to express my interest in his 1960 paper and asked rather naïvely if he had published related works (it turned out that he had indeed!). It was well over an hour later (probably closer to two) when I hung up the phone, but not before Don had invited me to visit him at Lehigh at my earliest convenience. That opportunity did not present itself until October 1989 when I spent three wonderful days in Bethlehem as Don generously shared with me his time, home, library, copy machine, and files of correspondence with acquaintances such as Karl Popper and Konrad Lorenz. He was enthusiastically supportive when I mentioned my plan of writing a book on what I would come to call "universal selection theory" (although he did cautiously inquire first if I was already tenured—fortunately, I was). After another visit to Bethlehem a year later, a meeting in Chicago, and countless telephone conversations and e-mail messages, my book, *Without Miracles: Universal Selection Theory and the Second Darwinian Revolution*, was finally published in 1995, less than a year before Don passed away.

While I could recount much more about my experiences with Don Campbell and his impact on me, the remainder of this chapter focuses on the substance of this impact. First, I present Campbell's view that all "puzzles of fit" owe their origin to a Darwinian process that he called "blind variation and selective retention" (BVSR). Campbell first referred to this thesis as "evolutionary epistemology" (Campbell, 1974b) but later preferred to call it "general selection theory" or "selection-theory epistemology," while I refer to it (and will do so in this chapter) as "universal selection theory" (UST). Second, I discuss the implications of UST for several different fields, with emphasis on neuroscience and cognitive psychology. I describe how in many different disciplines, discoveries have been made and methods are being used that are both consistent with and provide support for UST. Finally, in an attempt to clarify some of Campbell's key ideas concerning UST and to respond to his critics, I present a framework for considering the complementary roles of among-organism and within-organism BVSR as well as for the complementarity of prior and current BVSR in all instances of knowledge generation and growth.

Campbell's Universal Selection Theory

It is primarily due to Campbell that a general selection theory of the emergence of knowledge is known (and contested) today. Campbell has three major accomplishments to his credit in this regard. First, he documented the discovery and use of selectionist theories of thought by philosophers, psychologists, mathematicians, and other scientists since the time of Darwin (Campbell, 1974b). Second, over a period of more than 35 years he provided convincing (to some) and controversial (to others) arguments that the Darwinian process of BVSR underlies all achievements of fit. These achievements of fit include the fit of our perceptions to aspects of the world they represent, the fit of our thoughts and mental processes to the problems we confront and solve, and the fit of our scientific theories and predictions to the phenomena they describe. Finally, Campbell described a hierarchy of knowledge processes to explain how the emergence and growth of all forms of knowledge can be accounted for within a general selectionist framework (Campbell, 1974b).

Campbell's universal selection theory consists of four basic claims (1974b, p. 421):

1. A blind-variation-and-selective-retention process is fundamental to all inductive achievements, to all genuine increases in knowledge, to all increases in fit of system to environment.
2. In such a process there are three essentials: (a) mechanisms for introducing variation; (b) consistent selection processes; and (c) mechanisms for preserving and/or propagating the selected variations. Note that in general the preservation and generation mechanisms are inherently at odds, and each must be compromised.
3. The many processes which shortcut a more full blind-variation-and-selective-retention process are themselves inductive achievements, containing wisdom about the environment achieved originally by blind variation and selective retention.
4. In addition, such shortcut processes contain in their own operation a blind-variation-and-selective-retention process at some level, substituting for overt locomotor exploration or the life-and-death winnowing of organic evolution.

These are bold claims having important implications for our understanding of the genesis of all forms of knowledge. Claims 1 and 2, if true, would lead us to expect to find mechanisms of BVSR underlying all processes that result in the fit of one system to another, such as any form of adaptation. We now consider some examples from various disciplines that are consistent with Campbell's universal selectionism, with emphasis on recent developments in neuroscience and psychology.

Biological Evolution

Perhaps the most striking instances of fit are those demonstrated by the structure, physiology, and instinctive behavior of living organisms. In the 141 years since the publication of *The Origin of Species* many alternatives have been proposed, but Darwin's theory of natural selection involving the cumulative BVSR of organisms remains today the only nonmiraculous explanation for the emergence and evolution of species and their adaptive characteristics (see Cziko, 1995, chap. 2).

Immunology

The match of antibodies to antigen (such as pathological bacteria and viruses) achieved by the mammalian immune system constitutes another striking puzzle of fit. Many different theories for this puzzle have been proposed in the past (including the providential germ-line theory of Paul Ehrlich and the instructionist template theory of Linus Pauling). But today it is widely accepted that effective antibodies are produced by a process of within-organism BVSR, a theory known as the clonal-selection theory of antibody production (see Cziko, 1995, chap. 4).

Computer Science and Chemistry

There are also striking instances of fit to be found in the areas of computer science, chemistry, and pharmacology. One of the most exciting and promising topics in computer science in recent years has been the development of methods to generate computer programs able to perform a wide variety of tasks without explicit programming by a human programmer. These methods are collectively referred to as *evolutionary computing* and include the early efforts of Fogel and his associates (Fogel, Owens & Walsh, 1996), the use of *genetic algorithms* by Holland (1992), and the *genetic programming* of Koza (1992, 1994). All of these methods depend on the cumulative BVSR of segments of computer code using analogues of point mutation and/or sexual genetic recombination. In chemistry and pharmacology, similar methods are now employed in order to create new chemical compounds. *Directed molecular evolution* (see Joyce, 1992) and *combinatorial chemistry* (see Hall, 1997; Plunkett & Ellman, 1997) use cumulative blind variation of molecules followed by a process of filtering (selection) to derive molecules with desired functional shapes and properties, for example, the ability to bind with certain receptor sites in the body (see Cziko 1995, chaps. 13 and 14 for more information on evolutionary computing and the artificial selection of molecules).

Neuroscience

The fit of the mammalian brain to the body that houses it and to the perceptual and behavioral demands of survival and reproduction in complex environments is arguably the most striking puzzle of all. Understanding how something as complex as the human brain can develop from a single fertilized egg is a major challenge in neuroscience, as is understanding how the brain changes its structure to make memory and learning possible throughout a person's lifetime.

The adult human brain contains about 11 billion specialized nerve cells, or *neurons*, and each neuron may have up to 10,000 connections, called *synapses*, with other neurons. It is widely believed today by neuroscientists, psychologists, and even some philosophers, that all of the knowledge that the human brain contains—from knowing how to walk to being able to perform abstract scientific and mathematical reasoning—is a function of the brain's neurons and their interconnections. Therefore, understanding how the functional complexity of the brain develops is a major goal in the behavioral and brain sciences.

While it was thought at one time that the brain's complex organization was fully specified in the human genome as a result of many millions of years of natural selection, research findings now cast doubt on such a view. For one thing, it is estimated that the human neocortex alone (the most recent addition to our brain) has about 10^{15} (that is, one thousand million million) synapses (Eccles, 1989, pp. 1, 4). Since the entire human genome has only about 3.5 x 10^9 (3.5 billion) bits of information stored as nucleotide base pairs, some scientists (for example, Deacon, 1997, p. 197) have concluded that our genes simply don't have enough storage capacity to specify all of these connections, in addition to including information on the location and type of each neuron plus similar information for the rest of the brain.

How then is the brain able to achieve the very specific and adapted wiring required to function in so many remarkable ways? For example, how does a motor neuron know to which particular muscle fiber it should connect? How is a sensory neuron in the visual system able to connect itself to the correct cell in the visual cortex of the occipital lobe of the brain? If the genes do not provide this detailed neuron-to-neuron wiring plan, from where does it come?

It turns out that the precise wiring of the brain and nervous system is accomplished by a process that *eliminates* many neurons and synapses. As far back as 1906 it was discovered that of the 20,000 or so neurons present in a particular location of a chicken embryo's spinal cord, only about 12,000 remained in the adult chicken (Hamburger, 1975). In addition to entire neurons, countless synaptic connections are also eliminated during the development of a bird or mammal's nervous system.

But how does the nervous system know which connections to retain and which to eliminate? The work of Hubel and Wiesel in the 1970s (who shared a Nobel Prize in 1981) provided an important clue. They conducted their groundbreaking experiments by sewing closed the lid of one eye of newborn cats, and found that even one week without sight altered the neural connections of the eyes to the occipital cortex. Neurons carrying nervous signals from the closed eye made fewer connections with the cortex, whereas those from the open eye made many more connections than was normal.

This finding suggests that visual system neurons engage in a form of Darwinian competition for space in the visual cortex, with the result of the competition dependent on the amount and type of sensory stimulation carried by the axons.

We now understand that the normal development of the brain is a function of the *interaction* between genetic inheritance and environmental experience. The genome interacting with the organism's internal environment provides the general form of the brain while nervous system activity and sensory stimulation provide the means by which the brain is fine-tuned and made fully operational. But this fine-tuning does not depend on adding new components and connections in the way that a radio is normally assembled in a factory. Instead it is achieved by *eliminating* much of what was originally present. It is as if the radio arrived on the assembly line with twice as many electrical components and connections needed. If such an overconnected radio were plugged in and turned on, nothing but silence, static, or a hum would be heard from its loudspeaker. However, careful removal of unnecessary components and judicious snipping of redundant wires would leave just those components and connections that result in a functioning radio. This snipping is analogous to the elimination of synapses in the human brain as part of its normal development.

Greenough has studied in microscopic detail the process by which brain connections change over time as maturing animals interact with their environments. Using sophisticated techniques for determining the numbers of neurons and synapses in the rat's brains, he and his associates found a rapid spurt in the growth of synapses during the first months of life that occurs regardless of the amount or type of sensory experience (Greenough & Black, 1992). This period of synaptic "blooming" is followed by a sharp decline in the number of synapses. That is, an elimination or "pruning" of synapses then takes place based on the activity and sensory stimulation of the brain, ultimately resulting in the pattern of connections characteristic of the mature rat's brain. Greenough refers to this initial blooming and pruning of synapses as experience-expectant learning because the initial synaptic overproduction appears to be relatively independent of the animal's experiences. It is as though the brain is expecting important things to happen during the first weeks and months of life and so is prepared for these experiences with an overabundance of synapses, only a fraction of which will be selectively retained. While the work of Greenough and his associates has been limited to rats and monkeys, autopsies of human cortex have also found a decrease to about 60 percent of the maximum number of synapses as the human brain matures (Huttenlocher & Dabholkar, 1997, p. 167). In a recent book on the evolution of language, Deacon (1997, p. 199) summarizes the role of within-organism Darwinism in the brain:

> In the same sense that Darwinian processes have created new design information for building organisms during the course of the evolution of life, Darwinian-like processes in brain development are responsible for creating the new information required to adapt large brains to themselves and to their bodies.

Greenough's work has led him to propose a selectionist theory to account for the adult brain's ability to learn new skills and form new memories. According to this theory, *experience-dependent* learning involves both the addition and elimination of synapses. The addition involves the formation of new synapses in response to the animal's attempt to control aspects of a new, complex environment. Although the brain does appear to somehow know what part of itself to involve in this synapse construction project (as the result of prior among-organism selection and/or prior within-organism BVSR, as discussed in the final section), it need not (and most likely could not) know which particular individual connections to make. By forming a large variety and number of new connections, the brain can select the combinations that work best, in the same way that the immature, developing brain retains useful connections from its initial oversupply of synapses (referred to by Greenough as "experience-expectant learning"). The long-term result is an overall addition to the number of synapses. But the actual selection process that fine-tunes the connections is a subtractive one in which the useful connections are selectively retained and less useful ones eliminated.

Although clear evidence exists for synaptic increase in learning, we do not yet have clear evidence that mature learning involves an overproduction of synapses that are then pruned away. However, recent research has found evidence for an overproduction of dendrites in mature rats during readaptation of the brain after injury, indicating that the overproduction of synapases may be involved as well (Jones & Schallert, 1992, 1994; Schallert & Jones, 1993). These findings fit very nicely with the subtractive synapse findings on brain maturation and provide an elegant solution to the puzzle of how the brain could know exactly which new synaptic connections to establish to enable it to acquire new knowledge, skills, and memories.

A few years ago only a small number of neuroscientists ascribed to the view that the adult brain develops and learns through a process of cumulative neural BVSR. Today, however, such a view is starting to be considered mainstream, if still contested (see Quartz & Sejnowski, 1997, and following commentaries and response). Neuroscientist William Calvin refers to the brain as a "Darwin machine" that follows the plan of making lots of random variants by "brute bashing about," then selecting the good ones (1987; see also 1996a, 1996b). Edelman, who shared a Nobel Prize in 1972 for his research on the chemical structure of antibodies in the immune system, has written several books describing his neuronal group selection theory of brain development and learning that he refers to as neural Darwinism (1987, 1988, 1989, 1992).

Current research is under way to find physical evidence for the overproduction and elimination of newly formed synapses in the adult mammalian brain as the mechanism underlying learning. Newly developed brain imaging techniques such as magnetic resonance imaging are also being used to gain new insights into the functioning of the human brain. Finding clear evidence for BVSR in the structural modification and functioning of the brain would place it alongside the immune system as another striking example of how cumulative BVSR operating during the lifetime of an organism makes it possible to adapt to new and changing environments. As such, it would constitute impressive support for one important aspect of Campbell's UST.

Psychology

Although he was interested in all potentially BVSR-driven knowledge processes (which is one reason he possessed such impressive interdisciplinary knowledge), Campbell as a psychologist was primarily interested in the BVSR involved in human perception and cognition, particularly creativity and problem solving. When Campbell first proposed his selectionist theory to the field of psychology, he anticipated difficulty in finding empirical support, noting "the unfavorable ratio of hypothesized unobservable processes to observable input-output variables" (Campbell, 1960, p. 397). Thoughts and ideas do not leave fossils that can be dug up and examined, nor are they readily accessible to most other means of scientific observation and measurement. But now, almost forty years later, there is a growing body of evidence that some cognitive processes do involve the Darwinian BVSR of thought trials. Much of this research deals with human creativity and invention and has been reviewed by Simonton (1999a). Some of these studies will now be summarized.

If it is true that creativity and other adaptive forms of human creativity depend on the BVSR of thought trials, then we should expect that problem solving and creativity would be enhanced by factors that increase the variability and number of thoughts trials. This has been found in a number of experimental studies. Subjects in one study were provided with shapes and forms to create objects having certain functions (Finke, Ward & Smith, 1992). It was found that they came up with the best and most imaginative inventions when both the provided forms and target function were randomly selected from a large set of possibilities. In another study it was found that randomly generated associations facilitated problem solving on a marketing task (Proctor, 1993).

Other investigations, known as psychometric studies, have examined relationships between certain psychological traits and creativity. These studies have found that above a certain basic level, IQ is not related to creative ability (Simonton, 1985). Instead, creative individuals tend to produce many varied ideas (e.g., Eysenck, 1993, 1994, 1995). Indeed, tests that attempt to measure creativity typically do so not by replicating the types of items found on intelligence tests but rather by assessing an individual's ability to generate many diverse ideas. For example, the Remote Associations Test (Mednick, 1962) assesses creativity by measuring one's ability to create associations between dissimilar ideas. Other tests assess an individual's ability for what is called divergent thinking, that is, the ability to generate many novel and diverse responses to a problem or question. An example of such a test is the Alternate Uses Tests in which one attempts to come up with as many different uses for an object as one can.

Other aspects of personality that have been found to be associated with creativity also provide support for a within-organism Darwinian view of cognition. Simonton (1999a, p. 315) summarized this research by noting that:

> Creative personalities tend to possess those characteristics that would most favor the production of ideas both numerous and diverse. In particular, creative individuals tend to be independent, non-conformist, unconventional, even bohemian; they also tend to have wide interests, greater openness to new experiences, and a more conspicuous behavioral and cognitive flexibility and boldness.

Also of interest are studies of creativity and invention that use historical measures. Historiometric studies conducted by Simonton (1979, 1987, 1997) have shown that those individuals who are most prolific are also the most successful in creative achievements. This relationship between quantity and inventive success holds across as well as within individuals and thus suggests that creativity is a function of blind variations. The more an individual produces, the more likely he or she is to be successful in some creative endeavor. In similar manner, plant breeders often use mutagens such as radiation in order to increase the mutation rate to develop new cultivars with useful characteristics (this method was used to transform inedible rapeseed oil into the canola oil that is now found in many foods). Of particular interest is the finding that the proportion of produced variations that are successful does not increase as an individual gains experience in his or her field. Rather, individuals appear to be most creative around the age of 40, which is when they produce the greatest number of variations. It has also been argued that a Darwinian view of creativity accounts for the output of scientific communities who take the ideas proposed by individual scientists and continue to test and vary them, so much so that "the end product may solve a problem the originator of the idea has not dreamt about; in suggesting the idea, the originator was 'blind' to the problem that is eventually solved in the process he initiated" (Kantorovich, 1993, p. 198).

Finally, in the field of cognitive development, Siegler (1996) has found a high degree of variation in the problem-oriented thinking of children and argues that "variability and selection functions seem essential to any developing system. Thus, they may be a basic part of many, if not most, mechanisms of cognitive development" (Siegler, 1989, p. 376).

These are just a few of the studies from the considerable (and growing) body of empirical research that supports a within-organism BVSR theory of the creative thought and behavior consistent with Campbell's UST.

The Complementarity of Different Types of BVSR

The discovery of within-organism Darwinian processes involving cumulative BVSR has provided some clear answers and suggests others to a number of vexing problems concerning the functioning of the immune system, the processes involved in human thought and creativity, and the development and modification of the brain. Since these processes all involve some form of adaptation of one system to another, we should not be too surprised to learn that Darwinian processes of BVSR are involved in these phenomena. In effect, through the process of among-organism BVSR, mechanisms of within-organism BVSR have evolved allowing organisms to solve what Plotkin (1994, p. 135) has called the "uncertain futures problem."

But despite these findings and the "U" of UST, all neural and cognitive functioning need not involve BVSR. For example, while BVSR may be involved in the development of the human auditory system, once developed it appears to be able to directly and quickly analyze human speech sounds with remarkable accuracy with little if any "groping" or guessing. It seems that the among-organism BVSR of human evolution (along with, in the case of the auditory system, some fine tuning involving selective neuronal and synaptic elimination) has provided us with some systems that are able to function quite well without current on-going BVSR. This is included in Campbell's third claim above that recognizes the existence of "shortcuts" to full BVSR. But Campbell insisted (as would I) that systems facing continual challenges and new environments, such as the mammalian immune and nervous systems, must rely on on-going BVSR in order to adapt to these new circumstances (see his fourth claim above).

Among- and Within-Organism BVSR

A clearer understanding of the roles of among-organism and within-organism selection can be obtained by considering Figure 2.1 that displays the hypothesized relative importance of the two processes for three different types of behavioral knowledge. To the extreme left we have what are usually considered inborn instincts, such as the spider's weaving a web or a newly hatched gosling following the first large moving object it sees. Such behaviors are adaptations that may be entirely due (or nearly so) to the among-organism BVSR of biological evolution.

In the middle of Figure 2.1 we have knowledge in the form of adapted behavior that is not innate, but rather acquired during the lifetime of the individual. One obvious

Figure 2.1. Complementarity of Among-Organism and Within-Organism BVSR for Three Different Types of Behavioral Knowledge

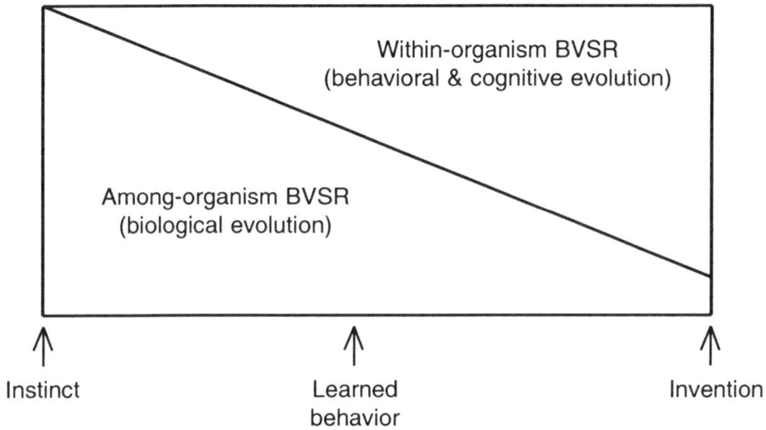

example is a rat learning to push a lever to obtain bits of food in a Skinner box. Here we have what appears to be the within-organism BVSR of behaviors emitted by the rat. But a better example for our present purpose is the type of learning studied by Köhler (1925) in apes, such as learning to stack two or more boxes to reach a suspended banana or use a stick to pull in a banana placed outside the ape's cage. Such learning often appears insightful; that is, after what appears to be a period of incubation, the ape proceeds directly to the solution with no overt BVSR of behaviors. Thanks to Campbell, we can understand such learning as the result of within-organism BVSR involving the generation, evaluation, and selection of thought trials that substitute for overt behaviors.

Note, however, that among-organism BVSR still plays an essential part in such learned behavior, as it is responsible for the ape having the necessary equipment (eyes, hands, arms, legs, brain) and motivation (a liking for bananas) for solving the problem. But now the among-organism BVSR of biological evolution is clearly not sufficient since, unlike instincts, what emerges is a new behavior that could not have been naturally selected in the ape's evolutionary past. Such acquired behavior involves both among-organism (biological) BVSR and within-organism (cognitive and/or behavioral) BVSR.

One way of conceptualizing the importance of among-organism BVSR (biological evolution) in learning is the degree to which it provides constraints for the generation of variations used by subsequent within-organism BVSR. For example, young children readily learn the meanings of words spoken to them by their caretakers (as rapidly as one word per waking hour). While biological evolution cannot provide the child with the meanings of these words (in the way that it may provide the meaning of a scream), it has set rather narrow (and very useful) limits on the possibilities that a child is willing to entertain. So while a young child may have little difficulty in learning the meanings of *hand*, *arm*, and *forearm*, (the latter referring to both the hand and arm up to around the elbow), she would not expect a single word to refer to both shoulder and hand, or to both knee and foot, or to both red and blue. Such constraints, the results of evolutionary among-organism BVSR, have the effect of usefully limiting or guiding the necessary within-organism BVSR that must take place to acquire a language (see Campbell, 1973).

Now we move to the extreme right of Figure 2.1. Here we find certain forms of knowledge (behavioral and/or cognitive adaptations) that appear to rely primarily on within-organism BVSR. Of course, among-organism BVSR must still play a role since biological brains and limbs are obviously involved (which is why in Figure 2.1 the line separating among-organism from within-organism selection never quite makes it to the lower right corner). But at this end there are fewer useful biological constraints on the within-organism BVSR. I have given human invention as an example of such an adaptation, since there are apparently few useful biologically evolved constraints for the variations that must be considered for inventing steam engines, light bulbs, transistors, or nuclear fusion reactors.

Prior and Current BVSR

The second important distinction with respect to BVSR is that between prior and current BVSR. Obviously, the among-organism BVSR of biological evolution is prior BVSR. But within-organism BVSR can be seen as either prior or current. An ape confronted for the first time with boxes and a suspended banana must engage in some form of current behavioral and/or cognitive BVSR to generate a solution for reaching the banana. But the ape who had already solved the task yesterday need use little or no current BVSR of behavioral or thought trials since the knowledge gained from yesterday's experiences remains to guide the ape today. Such prior BVSR can be useful even if the task is modified so that different boxes (e.g., boxes open on one end) are made available or a desired object other than a banana (e.g., a favorite toy) is suspended out of reach. As stated in Campbell's third claim, prior within-organism BVSR results in knowledge that can be used to usefully constrain current BVSR for similar types of tasks.

Figure 2.2 indicates the complementary role of prior BVSR and current BVSR for different types of behaviors or abilities. At the left end we find both instinctive (e.g., bird nest building) and well-learned behaviors (e.g., a pianist's playing a familiar musical piece). For such behaviors no cur-

Figure 2.2. Complementarity of Prior and Current BVSR for Three Different Types of Behavioral Knowledge

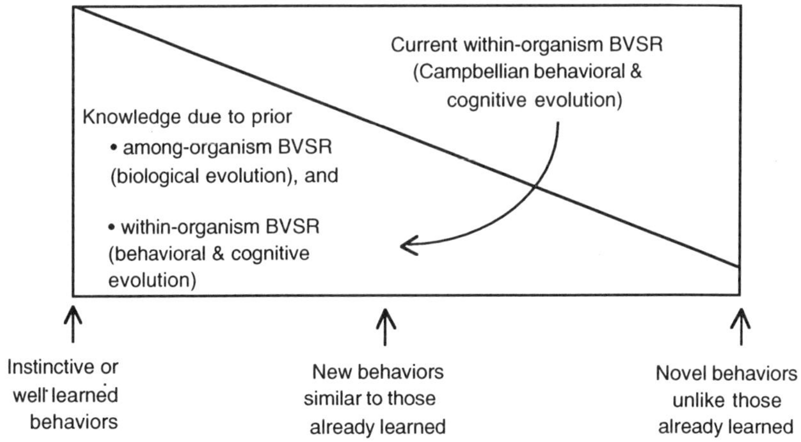

rent BVSR may be necessary for accomplishing the task. For instincts, among-organism BVSR supplies the necessary knowledge. For well-learned non-instinctive behaviors, it is a combination of among-organism BVSR and prior within-organism BVSR that provides the knowledge necessary for the new behavior or ability.

Moving toward the middle of Figure 2.2 we find behaviors and abilities similar to, but not identical to, those already acquired. Prior within-organism BVSR provides some of the knowledge necessary for these behaviors, but it is not sufficient thereby making additional current BVSR necessary for its achievement. Having created one successful musical composition or invention, one may find creating the next one quite a bit easier. But some additional current BVSR will be necessary if the next work is not to be just a copy or imitation of the previous one.

On the right of Figure 2.2 we find novel behaviors unlike those already learned. To learn such behaviors or develop new abilities, current BVSR must play a major role since little has already been learned to constrain or guide the new variations that must be generated and tested. The arrow in Figure 2.2 between "current within-organism BVSR" and "prior within-organism BVSR" indicates the transformation of current BVSR to knowledge that may be used to constrain future within-organism BVSR.

Conclusion

Recognizing the complementarity of among-organism and within-organism BVSR as well as of prior and current BVSR provides a useful perspective on Campbell's four claims concerning the universality of BVSR as underlying the emergence of all forms of knowledge. If, for example, an organism enters the world already knowing how to perform a complex behavior (such as those involved in finding food, defending oneself, and mating), such knowledge is the result of the among-organism BVSR of biological evolution. If, however, new behaviors are learned following new environmental demands (such as a seal learning to balance a beach ball on its nose to obtain food from its trainer, or a physicist developing a new superconducting material), such new knowledge involves in addition within-organism BVSR.

This framework can be used to address the arguments of some critics of Campbell's UST. One criticism is that evolution has endowed our species with sensory and mental abilities that make it possible for us to acquire new knowledge without resorting to the stupid and wasteful process of BVSR (see, for example, Bradie's 1986 distinction between the evolutionary epistemology of *mechanisms* and the evolutionary epistemology of *theories*). Another related criticism is that the behavioral, perceptual, and cognitive variations generated by creative, problem-solving human beings are not blindly produced but rather intelligently directed toward the problem solution or desired invention (see, for example, Thagard, 1988, p. 103). But as Campbell has emphasized repeatedly (for example, see Campbell, 1990b, p. 9), if the variations an organism generates appear knowledgeable there must be an explanation for this knowledge. And BVSR (both among- and within-organism) is currently the only sufficiently stupid process with a proven track record for generating new knowledge to provide a satisfactory nonmiraculous explanation.

This does not mean, however, that BVSR must *necessarily* be found to be a part of all adaptive and knowledge-generating processes and therefore UST constitutes an analytic, unfalsifiable truth (see Bradie, this volume). If a cold virus is introduced into my lungs by way of a coworker's sneeze, my body responds by producing antibodies that will eventually destroy all copies of the virus. If a slice of pizza finds its way into my stomach, my body responds by extracting the nutrients it contains and eliminating that which is not nutritive. In each case we observe a remarkably well-adapted and functional response. But while current BVSR is an essential part of the immune response, it apparently plays no role in digestion. As Pinker (1997, p. 210) has pointed out, "the stomach . . . does not randomly secrete variants of acids and enzymes, retain the ones that break down food a bit, let them sexually recombine and reproduce, and so on for hundreds of thousands of meals."

Thus a BVSR theory of digestion (if it has ever been seriously considered) has been falsified as this process has been found to function without cumulative variation and selection (although, of course, prior among-organism BVSR for the origin of the digestive system and its behavior is not so easily discounted). In contrast, a BVSR theory of antibody generation has not been falsified since it is not only consistent with what is currently known about the functioning of the mammalian immune system, but provides explanations for what are otherwise quite puzzling findings (see Cziko, 1995, chap. 4). It is only very recently that BVSR theories of brain functioning, synaptogenesis, problem solving, and creativity have begun to be formulated and tested, and decisive findings in these areas may prove elusive. We can nonetheless expect that many such theories will eventually be proposed and tested as additional BVSR-inspired research in these areas is conducted.

It is my hope that both Don Campbell's friends and critics (including those found between the covers of this volume) will find Figures 2.1 and 2.2 and their accompanying arguments useful in achieving a better understanding of UST and its potential application to all forms of knowledge generation. But no matter how useful this perspective may turn out to be, I know that I can never come close to fully repaying Don for all that he has given me and others who continue to seek nonmiraculous explanations for life, its marvelous design, and all the subsequent knowledge that life in its varied forms has generated and continues to create.

3

The Metaphysical Foundation of Campbell's Selectionist Epistemology

MICHAEL BRADIE

Introduction

I first came across Donald Campbell's work when I read his piece on "Evolutionary Epistemology" in the Schilpp volume on Karl Popper. What struck me in particular about Campbell's article was the comment by Popper that there was "the almost complete agreement, down to even minute details, between Campbell's views and my own" (Schilpp, 1974, p. 1059). Since the bulk of Popper's often churlish and acrimonious comments bemoaned the manner in which he was misunderstood and misrepresented by both critics and supporters alike, this tribute to Campbell was like a breath of fresh air. Some time later, in 1977 I think, I had occasion to return to Campbell's idea. I was called upon to give a talk to an undergraduate philosophy club at Bowling Green and was desperate for a topic. At the last minute, I came up with the idea of talking about the theory of natural selection as a model for Popper's conjectures and refutations model of scientific growth. Campbell's paper resurfaced in my memory. I subsequently wrote the paper and tried, unsuccessfully, to get it published.

In the meantime, I read an announcement of Campbell's request for papers on "evolutionary epistemology," published or not, for a comprehensive bibliography that he was compiling on the subject. I sent him the paper and Campbell wrote back with some papers of his own, along with a partial bibliography and words of encouragement. I soon realized that if this project was going to get off the ground, a careful articulation of the analogies or structural similarities between biological evolution and the growth of human knowledge was needed. All the material I had read, including my own first effort, contained only suggestive metaphors and sketchy models. This led me on a course of research that culminated in the paper "Assessing Evolutionary Epistemology," which was first presented at a meeting of the International Society for the History, Philosophy and Social Studies of Biology at Notre Dame in 1986.

I first met Campbell the following year at a conference in Australia. I found him to be warm, generous, and encouraging, even though he was not convinced by my attempt to bifurcate the evolutionary epistemology program into two separate projects. In subsequent years he was equally supportive.

In this chapter I propose to assess the development of Campbell's view on evolutionary epistemology or, as he came to prefer, selective epistemology. Section 2 contains a discussion of Campbell's development and a critical evaluation of some of the key features of his view. Section 3 provides a critical articulation of what I take to be the core metaphysical image underlying Campbell's epistemology. Finally, in the last section, I offer some conjectures about the future prospects for the development of evolutionary epistemology.

From Evolutionary to Selectionist Epistemology

Evolutionary models of conceptual change are complex and many faceted. In Bradie (1986) I distinguished two different, albeit interrelated, programs laying claim to being "evolutionary epistemologies." Although Campbell came to reject this analysis and urge that both exemplified an application of a "selectionist" model to epistemology, I remain convinced of the utility of the distinction. Since I will use it in my analysis of Campbell's position, I take this opportunity to restate it. The two programs are [1] EEM—the evolution of (biological or psychological) epistemic mechanisms, and [2] EET—the evolution of epistemic theories, by which I mean to include knowledge corpuses and epistemic norms. So the question of how human beings evolved to possess the capacities for higher intellectual thought including the ability to formulate scientific theories is an EEM project. The question of how, given those capacities, our knowledge of the external world has "evolved" is an EET project. I turn now to a sketch of the development of Campbell's "selectionist" epistemology.

The historical roots of Campbell's views lie in the nineteenth century philosophers Alexander Bain, William James, and J. M. Baldwin. Bain is credited with first describing learning as a "trial and error" process. William James is credited with the first explicit use of the evolutionary analogy to characterize thinking. While critical of Lamarckian views that the environment directly affects what we think and believe, Campbell notes that James "is surprisingly unobservant as to the details of the selection process, treating it as though all the selecting were being done by encounters with the external world, neglecting the vicarious editorial processes, conscious as well as unconscious" (Campbell, 1974c, p. 155). Baldwin (1909) is cited as source of the term "selection theory" (Campbell, 1974c, p. 144). Baldwin, James, and the other Darwinians are singled out by Campbell for battling the "Lamarckian" idea that evolution involved "foresight" or an assessment by the organism of its "needs."

The immediate inspiration for Campbell's initial foray into evolutionary models of learning and development came not from the biologists or psychologists but from the cyberneticists Ross Ashby and J. W. S. Pringle (Campbell 1956a, 1956b; Ashby 1952; Pringle 1951). In these two 1950s papers, Campbell sought to apply the trial-and-error model he found in Ashby's discussion of the design of a mechanical brain to problems of learning, habit formation and perception. Adaptive problems of biology and psychology can be posed either as phylogenetic or as ontogenetic problems. In the context of epistemology, ontogenetic issues concern the learning strategies and development of habits and epistemic practices of individual organisms. The phylogenetic issues focus on the accumulation of adaptive strategies across generations. This distinction cuts across the EEM/EET distinction.

In his second 1956 paper on the subject, Campbell addresses "the problem of adaptive fit in the execution of habits or instincts" in an individual organism (Campbell, 1956b, p. 334). The solution turns on the recognition that perception serves as a vicarious trial and error selector. Organisms use their perceptual modalities to sample their environments and modify their behavior accordingly. For human beings, the predominant modality is vision. Near the end of the article, Campbell points out the evolutionary significance of the correlation between reflective properties and imperviousness for the phylogenetic emergence of visual systems as surrogate exploratory devices:

> In the particular physical world in which we live and in which evolution took place, objects that are impervious to locomotion in general also reflect or diffuse certain electromagnetic waves. This persistent ecological condition over the eons has made possible the development of organisms able to anticipate the presence and location of solid objects through a substitute exploration based upon the opaqueness of the object to light. In the evolutionary perspective, vision is based upon this environmental correlation, as is our recent development of radar. The austere logical environment of [Ashby's] Homeostat lacks such fortunate coincidences. No environmental parameters are provided which are correlated to other environmental parameters so highly that search of one can substitute for trial and error in contact with the other. (Campbell, 1956b, p. 340)

This account provides a "phylogenetic" analysis of the development of a physiological mechanism (vision) that organisms come to rely on in the formation of habits during their lifetimes. In short, Campbell's first excursions into evolutionary epistemology address what I would characterize as EEM problems. The formation of habits in individual organisms I would classify as an ontogenetic EEM problem. The evolution of vision into a vicarious trial and error modality is a phylogenetic EEM problem. The extension of this analysis to what I would call EET concerns occurs in Campbell (1959).

Campbell cites, with approval, Herbert Feigl's contention that there is an essential sameness between rats learning mazes and "intellectual adaptations . . . of the Newtons, Maxwells, and Einsteins" (Campbell, 1959, p. 153). This characterization marks an extension of the trial and error model to the characterization of the products of human theorizing. This is EET territory. Intellectual adaptations can be viewed from both an ontogenetic and a phylogenetic perspective. Newton's "adaptations" as he struggled to formulate the principles of mechanics are parts of the ontogenetic history of the emergence of classical mechanics. That theory, seen as a precursor to Maxwell's theory, the theory of relativity and quantum mechanics, is one stage in the phylogenetic history of the development of scientific knowledge. This move involves a significant and dubious shift to which I will return.

Campbell sees his project as moving from the philosophy of science, with its then [1959] focus on conceptual analysis and the logic of science, to the construction of an empirical science of science grounded in psychological and sociological analyses of science (Campbell, 1959, p. 154). The purpose, he avers, is "to sketch out a hierarchy of knowledge processes at various biological levels, to examine these for recurrent attributes and differences, and then, considering science as one aspect of a general knowledge process, to make suggestions of tactics in the attempt to build a social science" (Campbell, 1959, p. 155). This is basically the model that emerges in Campbell's 1974 signature paper on evolutionary epistemology.

Campbell notes here that philosophers are specialists in "man the knower." As such, he thinks, they should be interested in the *empirical* aspects of knowing as well as the *conceptual* aspects (Campbell, 1959, p. 155). This is an early statement of the complementarian position that Campbell adopts with respect to the relationship between traditional epistemology and evolutionary or selectionist epistemology.

The Blind Variation and Selective Retention (BVSR) Model

Campbell's (1960) begins with a clear statement of his mature view:

> A blind-variation-and-selective-retention process is fundamental to all inductive achievements, to all genuine increases in fit of system to environment. (Campbell, 1960, p. 380)

Campbell allows as how he is employing an "extended usage" of the term "knowledge." In an extended footnote (Campbell, 1960, fn 2, p. 380) Campbell acknowledges that this extended usage is "part of an effort to put 'the problem of knowledge' into a behavioristic framework which takes full cognizance of man's status as a biological product of an evolutionary development from a highly limited background, with no 'direct' dispensations of knowledge being added at any point in family tree. . . . the position limits one to an 'epistemology of the other one.' The 'primitives' of knowledge can not be sought in 'raw feels' or in 'phenomenal givens,' or in any 'incorrigible' elements. While man's conscious knowledge processes are recognized as more complex and subtle than those of lower organisms, they are not taken as more fundamental or primitive. *In this perspective, any process providing a stored program for organismic adaptation in external environments is included as a knowledge process, and any gain in the adequacy of such a program is regarded as a gain in knowledge* [italics added]. If the reader prefers, he can understand the paper adequately regarding the term 'knowledge' as *metaphorical when applied to the lower levels in the development hierarchy* [italics added]. But since the problem of knowledge has resisted any generally accepted solution when defined in terms of the conscious contents of the philosopher himself, little seems lost and possibly something gained by thus extending the range of processes considered."

Blind variation is here taken to mean no foresight or prescience. Three essential connotations are noted: (1) The responses are not coupled to the environmental conditions or occasion of their emission. (2) The individual trial responses are uncorrelated with the solution (Campbell, 1960, p. 381). Campbell notes that this does not accurately describe how organisms do, in fact, behave. This discrepancy is taken not as a reflection of the inadequacy of the model but rather as an indication that the organism is making use of prior knowledge which in turn was generated by a BVSR process. (3) Successive responses are not corrections of earlier ones (Campbell, 1960, p. 381). Again the fact that organisms don't behave this way is not taken as a failure of the model but as an indication that BVSR processes are operating at other levels to produce heuristics for use in environmental probing.

Although the BVSR model has "unequivocal empirical implications, the major advantage to it may be metaphysical, or at least metatheoretical. Like the theory of natural selection in organic evolution, it provides an understanding of marvelously purposive processes without the introduction of teleological metaphysics or of pseudo-causal processes working backward in time" (Campbell, 1960, p. 396).

Notwithstanding all its virtues, Campbell is sensitive to the problems that face the view (Campbell, 1960, p. 396f). Some are shared with the theory of biological evolution but one major worry plagues the BVSR model. In order to make the "blind variation" theme work as a model of human intellectual activity, Campbell postulates a number of different hierarchically interconnected "levels" where BVSR processes are at work. The net result is a high ratio of "hypothesized unobservable processes" that need to be invoked to account for creative thinking. Campbell isolates several of them (Campbell, 1960, p. 397) and alleges that, with some controls, rigorous predictions that are potentially falsifiable can be made on the basis of the model. I am somewhat dubious of this claim since, as Campbell himself notes, the problem is in knowing that the relevant variables can be and are controlled. But without a clearer understanding of the underlying hypothetical processes and some assurance that we can empirically determine what they are doing, this is a problematic venture.

Nonetheless, Campbell notes that there are "unequivocal predictions regarding the volume and heterogeneity of thought trials" (Campbell, 1960, p. 397). "*Ceterus paribus*," he writes, "a creative solution is more likely the longer a problem is worked upon, the more valuable the thought trials, the more people working on the problem independently, the more heterogeneous these people, the less the time pressure, etc." (Campbell, 1960, p. 396). Conceding for a moment that these are indeed predictions of the BVSR model, the question remains whether these "predictions" represent "crucial experiments" that other accounts of creative thinking (or common sense) would not lead us to expect. These "predictions" do not have the character of "unexpected results" which is characteristic of the best tests of any empirical theory. However, are they really *predictions* of the model at all? One can see, more or less, how it is plausible that they should be, but this sense of plausibility is a result of a generous interpretation of what is, at this stage at least, a sketch of a theory. I daresay the intervening 38 years have not produced a version of the view that is much more articulate. More hard work at the empirical level in addition to a more specific articulation of the BVSR model is needed before we can be convinced that it is as testable as Campbell thought.

Evolutionary Epistemology as Descriptive Epistemology

Traditional epistemology focuses on issues concerning the definition of knowledge and its validation. Campbell calls this approach "analytic" epistemology. Philosophers traditionally ignore the details of how organisms come to acquire knowledge on the grounds that such empirical investigations can have no foundational significance, since they presuppose that we already understand what knowledge is. This neglected arena is the grist for Campbell's epistemological mill. He characterizes his approach as "descriptive" epistemology.

Unlike the traditional approach, which Campbell sees as attempting a transcendental analysis of the concept of knowledge that does not rely itself on any knowledge, the descriptive approach begins with human beings *in medias res* and takes the results of the special sciences as approximately correct. From this fallible starting point, the descriptive epistemologist seeks to formulate a theory about how organisms come to know the things that they do. Insofar as the traditional epistemologist is concerned to justify that knowledge is possible, the descriptive approach appears to be begging the question. And Campbell concedes that this approach does beg the traditional epistemologist's question. But that is not relevant, he argues, since the descriptive epistemologist is concerned with the (mainly empirical) details of how organisms evolved to become knowers at all and how it is that they come to know what they do (Campbell, 1974c, p. 140–41).

The fundamental stance of the descriptive epistemologist is what Campbell calls the "epistemology of the other one." Having abandoned the classical epistemologist stance of trying to produce a theoretical account of knowledge that is not itself dependent on any (empirical) knowledge (at least), the descriptive epistemologist abandons the Cartesian project of trying to ground all knowledge on the immediate self-evident intuitions of the knowing subject. The descriptive epistemologist starts from the presumption that he or she is an (imperfect) knower and focuses on other individuals and how they come to know what they do. In the light of what we learn about others, we come to have views about what and how we know ourselves, but of course these views can never free themselves from the initial presumptions we used to start our inquiry. So knowledge is always presumptive, partial, hypothetical and fallible (Overman, 1988, p. 445).

Descriptive epistemology is committed, on Campbell's view, to two metaphysical theses in addition to the methodological thesis of focusing on the "other one": (1) epistemological dualism and (2) critical or hypothetical realism.

Epistemological dualism is the thesis that our beliefs are distinct from their referents. Such a view allows the notion of "fit" to operate but of course since we can only compare beliefs or bits of knowledge with other beliefs and other bits of knowledge, the fit is inferred from the way our beliefs hang together.

Critical realism is the thesis that an external reality exists. It corresponds, for Campbell, to the biologist's distinction between organism and environment (Campbell, 1974c, 141). Just as the physical environment "shapes" the evolution of organismic features, so the physical environment is held to "shape" the evolution of what we know. But, I submit, there is a deep disanalogy between the two cases that undermines the attempts to lump together the evolution of organismic traits with the evolution of great ideas. In the former case, one might plausibly argue that the physical environment does indeed "shape" the development of physical characters. I concede this with some reservation, since the model on which it rests presupposes a sharp distinction between organism and environment. Campbell, in this discussion, takes it for granted that such a presupposition is part and parcel of every evolutionary biologist's understanding of how natural selection works. But Richard Lewontin (1982) has challenged the Cartesian metaphor on which this analysis rests. However, laying aside this reservation, the case of intellectual evolution is radically different. The picture that Campbell relies on presumes that beliefs are matched against the world and that the "fitter" beliefs prevail. But this picture ignores the fact that what we actually do (as Campbell himself has noted) is compare beliefs with other *beliefs*. These other *beliefs* are comprised of an environment of *data* and a range of *selective criteria*. That the world, in its brute facticity, plays *some* role in selecting out beliefs is not the issue. So one would be ill advised to try to fly out of a third story window by flapping one's arms despite what ideology one may believe. Nevertheless, complex bodies of theoretical knowledge are products of criterial presumptions which render suspect any model that takes them to be more or less directly reflective of the "shape of reality."

"The natural selection epistemology here offered has one special analytic feature: if one is expanding knowledge beyond what one knows, one has no choice but to explore without benefit of wisdom (gropingly, blindly, stupidly, haphazardly). This is an analytic truth central to all descriptive epistemologies of the natural selection variety" (Campbell, 1974c, p. 142). If indeed it is an analytic truth, then natural selection epistemologies preclude even the *possibility* that we don't always explore gropingly, blindly, stupidly or haphazardly. It is true that the BVSR model claims that, in *fact*, all expansions of knowledge beyond what is known are groping, blind, stupid, or haphazard, but it is not clear why it must be so. In fact, Campbell admits that appearances suggest that expansions of knowledge are *not completely* groping, blind, stupid, or haphazard. His response, as we noted above, is to argue that what appears directed at one level is the result of blind variation and selective retention at another level. But if the thesis is *analytic*, then that claim rests not so much on what the facts of the matter tell us but what is, in effect, a demand of the theory. The theory is thereby rendered unfalsifiable. Surely as descriptive epistemologists we want it to remain an open and empirical question whether or not such mechanisms exist at all the relevant knowing levels of organisms. It should also be an empirical question whether such mechanisms are a product of a phylogenetic history of blind variation and selective retention. If not, it is hard to see how one can construe selectionist accounts of the growth of knowledge as "explanatory."

One objection that is frequently raised against naturalized epistemologies in general and natural selection epistemologies in particular is that there is no room for an account of epistemic norms on such views. Such views, in Kim's words, are "epistemologies in name only" (Kim, 1988; cf Bradie, 1994, 1997). Campbell is sensitive to this objection and insists that his interests are "decidedly normative" as well as descriptive (Campbell, 1988f, p. 374). In the William James Lectures, presented in 1977, Campbell maintained that despite its focus on the empirical question of how organisms come to have knowledge, descriptive epistemology is *hypothetically* normative. Part of its task is to produce a theory about why certain practices, such as science, produce knowledge and other practices do not, and "how one should go about . . . [doing science] . . . if one wants valid knowledge" (Overman, 1988, p. 444). Campbell does not go into detail about what this "hypothetical" normativity amounts to but I am sympathetic to this line of thought. If one construes knowledge along Quinean lines as a holistic product of norms and experience, then just as our knowledge *claims* are conjectural and subject to revision so the *norms* we employ to validate them can be construed as conjectural and subject to revision as well (cf. Bradie, 1997).

The Metaphysical Foundations of Campbell's Selectionist Epistemology

At the heart of Campbell's view is a metaphysical picture or metaphor. It is the "insight" that scientists exploring the world are essentially no different from rats learning a maze (Campbell, 1960, 1982a). In this section I want to explore this metaphor and raise some crucial objections to it.

In his 1982 tribute to Baldwin, Campbell carefully distinguishes what he calls Baldwin's "critical realist instrumentalism" from Simmel's and James's pragmatism. The key, for Campbell, is that the pragmatic position downplays the distinction between Subject and Object where the Critical Realist position hinges on it. There is, according to Campbell, a "clear-cut distinction between organismic form and environmental characteristics [between Subject and Object] which is essential in evolutionary theory" (Campbell, 1982a, p. 94). This distinction, Campbell claims, "entails a parallel distinction between organismic behavior patterns and environment, and organismic cognitive maps, beliefs, etc. and environment" (Campbell, 1982a, p. 94).

I want to raise two issues here: (1) Is the "clear-cut distinction" essential in evolutionary theory? and (2) even if it were, does it "entail" the other two distinctions? My suggestion is that the answer to both questions is "No." I do not want to stop and argue against the first claim that such a distinction is "essential" to evolutionary theory. I refer the reader to Lewontin's paper which argues for a "dialectical" interpretation of the interrelationship between [organismic] subjects and [environmental] objects (Lewontin, 1982). But even if it were true that evolutionary theory did essentially rely on such a metaphysical claim, the "parallel" distinctions would not follow. To think that they would is to fail to appreciate the differences between EEM projects and EET projects.

What is driving the contention that there is no crucial difference between EEM projects and EET projects is the slippery notion of "shaping." We can all understand how the action of water and wind, for example, can shape a rock. It is a short step, one might think, to understand the evolution of a lineage as a similar process whereby a series of environmental interactions "shapes" the development of nervous systems, brains and perhaps inherited psychological dispositions. It seems just one further small step to understand the development of our cognitive maps, beliefs, and theories as the product of "shaping" by the (postulated) relatively stable external world. However, this last step, I contend, crosses a metaphysical divide that we need not traverse. Those who argue, as Campbell does, that we are compelled to do so are caught in the grip of a faulty picture—that just as organisms evolve to "fit" their environments, so our scientific theories evolve to "fit" the world. "For epistemology, the 'puzzles of fit' are to be found in the fit of beliefs to referent" (Campbell, 1990b, p. 2). These puzzles do not appear to everyone. The selection type theory is addressed to those who see a puzzle. But what exactly are these puzzles? There is an implicit analogy at work here—that organismic adaptations : environment : : belief : referent. How compelling is the analogy?

It is telling that Campbell endorses the project which led Bertrand Russell, in *Human Knowledge*, to his "Structural Postulates" (Russell, 1948). As Campbell sees it, the point is to triangulate on objects by fixing on a number of independent causal lines which lead back to the object under investigation. The robust consilience of these independent lines generates confidence in our beliefs about the object under investigation (Campbell, 1985, p. 57). This is characteristic of distal knowing where our techniques are often indirect and inferential. "Science," according to Campbell, " is the most distal form of knowing. Scientific theories are distal achievements" (Campbell, 1985, p. 63). What is telling about this endorsement is that Russell, in formulating those postulates, drew upon causal interactions between elements in the world of experience to use as a model for constructing a metaphysical picture of the relationship between a knowing subject and the world as it is "in itself." In Kantian terms, it is as if one were to use the experiential relationships of the phenomenal realm as a model for the relationship between the noumenal realm and the phenomenal realm. The "shaping" of rocks by their environments and lineages by their environments are facts to be determined in the phenomenal realm. The "shaping" of theories by the "world" is akin to the "shaping" of our phenomenal experience by the noumenal realm. The bottom line is that selectionist accounts of conceptual change that rely on the alleged "fit" between beliefs and the world do no more work for us in accounting for why we believe what we do than Kant's invocation of the noumenal realm did for him in accounting for why our phenomenal experiences are as they are.

In this regard, it is interesting to note that Campbell did, at least once, endorse the EEM/EET distinction (Campbell and Paller, 1989, p. 241). There are two agendas for EET as they see it: (1) To develop a naturalistic theory of "fit" between beliefs and the world; (2) To serve as a model for conceptual change. Of the two agendas for EET, they take the EET(1) agenda as primary. They see the basic task of selectionist epistemologies as that of explaining the puzzling fit between beliefs and the world. They recognize that the selective agency of the "invisible physical world" is but one of many factors determining which beliefs are selected and which not. However, they claim, "it is the only one directly relevant to the 'design' puzzle of increasingly competent reference" (Campbell and Paller, 1989, p. 242). In this regard, they take the parallels with biological natural selection to be only suggestively relevant. Since the term "evolutionary" is too suggestive of biological evolution, they prefer the term "selectionist epistemology."

The parallel to biological natural selection may only be "suggestively relevant" for a selectionist model of conceptual change, but it seems undeniable that the appeal of the epistemological puzzle, the force by which it captures our imagination, as it were, derives from our alleged recognition that the epistemic puzzle is just a natural extension of the biological puzzle. As such it rests on the dubious analogy: organisms or organismic traits/environment-beliefs/world.

Correlated with this metaphysical picture is a commitment to a correspondence theory of truth and what Campbell calls a "correspondence goal of science." Our beliefs are true when they "fit" the world and it is the aim of science to produce a systematic body of such cohering beliefs whose mutual reinforcement provides us with the evidence that, indeed, they do (more or less) "fit" the world. So our aim is to discover truths that correspond to reality but our best, albeit fallible, test of these truths is their coherence. Coherence is a "symptom" of truth not its definition. Campbell is well aware of the long dialectical struggle between these two conceptions of truth, but instead of fruitlessly stopping to engage these issues, chooses to cut the Gordian knot and move on.

As I understand him, this fundamental commitment is not something that is subject to revision in the light of scientific advances and the consequent reshuffling of knowledge corpora and our other epistemic commitments. Thus, Campbell's project appears to be wedded to a particular picture of the human epistemic predicament. When we challenge that picture and its underlying metaphor, the puzzles that emerge from it lose some of their seemingly intrinsic compellingness.

Campbell thinks that the presence of the real world as ultimate selector is what distinguishes science and its evolution from other social belief systems and their evolution. And, prejudiced as it may be, I share Campbell's conviction that science and scientific practices differ in fundamental ways from, say, religion and religious practices or superstitions and superstitious practices. But part of the difference between them is in their respective aims. The aim of science, to put it as neutrally as possible, is to provide an understanding of how things work. The aim of religion and superstitions, one might suggest, is primarily to provide aid and comfort to the distressed. Sometimes religion and superstition venture to give an account of how things work in the process of fulfilling their primary function. When there is a conflict between the accounts (Feyerabendian animadversions aside), science and its practices trump religion and superstition. So if the point is to produce some beliefs about the regularity with which the sacred volcano erupts then, in a closed bid competition, we would be mightily surprised if the best vulcanologist's predictions, which for the sake of the example we will assume closely matches the actual eruption pattern, were matched as well by the predictions of the competitors. Of course, we don't *now* know how to predict the frequency and regularity underlying volcano eruptions and so present day scientific predictions are likely to be no better than the others. But if we had to place a bet on which practice would first come up with a reasonably accurate predictive strategy in such a case, my bet, at least, would be on the scientists. However, I do not think that commits me to accepting the metaphysical picture that underlies Campbell's view, even if I were to endorse some form of a variation and selective retention model for describing the progress of science.

How, then, one might ask, are we to explain the *success* of science? Well, that question can be given a *local* or a *global* twist. From a local point of view, we want to understand the success, such as it was, of discarded theories. How could Newtonian mechanics, for example, have survived as long as it did given our present convictions that it is a fundamentally incorrect picture of the world? The local answer is that the successor theories, Einstein's theories of relativity, contain within themselves the ability to account for the success of Newton's theory. In the ordinary course of our experience, at least up until the twentieth century, the differences between what we are led to expect on the two theories is experimentally undetectable (with one or two possible exceptions that, in the nineteenth century as the Newtonian framework was beginning to crack, were taken to be anomalies). From a global point of view, where what we want to explain is the success of science *per se* as opposed to the success of this or that particular theory, I contend that, once we discard the image upon which Campbell's position rests, there is nothing left to explain. If the question is why the practices collectively known as "scientific" produce the kinds of results they do while the practices of the other belief systems do not produce the *same* kinds of results, I am not sure that I have any better answer than: they just don't! But I remain unconvinced that Campbell's metaphysical appeal to the image of beliefs "fitting" to reality helps.

Conclusion

I have argued that Campbell's selectionist account of the evolution of scientific knowledge rests on a dubious metaphysical picture. This picture of beliefs "fitting" to the world provides only the semblance of an explanation of the "success" of science. Nonetheless, it still may be true that a selection theory may serve as an appropriate model for scientific change as envisaged in the second EET agenda endorsed by Campbell and Paller.

In response to a criticism by Peter Medawar to the effect that the disanalogies between biological evolution and the evolution of ideas are greater than the analogies, Campbell reaffirms his commitment to a BVSR model as applied to thinking and notes that the "absence of any conceivable alternative is an important determinant of [his] . . . faith" in its applicability to this case (Campbell, 1974c, p. 161). He notes that much of the "blind permuting" might take place unconsciously, and so would not be noticeable to us as we reflect on how we think. This, of course, removes the possibility of a phenomenological test of the applicability of the model. But if the model is correct and the relevant processes are for the most part unconscious, then a vindication of its applicability rests on detailed neurological models of the workings of our brains (Campbell, 1974c, p. 161). So there is an empirical project for the future to test the empirical adequacy of Campbell's selectionist epistemology. But, I daresay, this is a project for the distant future given our inadequate understanding of the workings of the human brain not to mention the connection between those workings and our conceptual schemes.

In his later papers, Campbell expresses sensitivity to the relevance of social factors in determining the "fit" between our ideas and the world. He criticizes the evolutionary models of conceptual change in science as developed by Toulmin, Hull, and Richards, for example, for failing to take into account the fact that, in addition to being tested against "nature," there are other selective factors at work in determining which ideas survive and which do not. This is the legacy of the social constructionist critiques of the concept of scientific objectivity. It is not clear how Campbell thinks his model can do any better. Merely stipulating that "presumptive tests against nature" or the importance of "demonstrations" are at the heart of the development of scientific knowledge won't do unless there is a clear and unambiguous method of disentangling the influence of socially constructed norms upon the very ideas of "tests against nature" and "demonstration." And at least part of the force of social constructionist critiques, I take it, is to call into question this very possibility. Campbell's view, on the other hand, seems to take it for granted that there is a clear-cut distinction between norms that validate the "fit" between beliefs and *objective* referents and those that legitimize beliefs by validating a "fit" between the beliefs and some *merely* socially constructed standards.

Attempting to locate the EEM and EET programs under a single "selectionist" rubric obscures what I take to be fundamental differences between the two projects. The EET schemas are in danger of becoming empty formalisms. Even if the empirical agenda succeeds, the metaphysical agenda remains suspect. The metaphysical foundation of Campbell's analysis rests on a dubious picture that is not at all obviously required by any analysis that attempts to explain the "progress" of science.

4

Critical Hypothetical Evolutionary Naturalism

Ronald N. Giere

Campbell's Naturalism

Among philosophers, Don Campbell is best known for his naturalistic, evolutionary approach to epistemology. There can be no doubt, however, that he was a thoroughgoing naturalist in all matters, even though he seems to have had little interest in exploring naturalism as a general philosophical position. He was professionally more interested in the origins and workings of knowledge producing social systems. I am interested in these things too, but also naturalism in general. So my tribute to Don will be to present some aspects of a generalized naturalism that I hope he would have liked.

Campbell's naturalism, like his epistemology, would be *evolutionary*, but, like his realism, would be more. It would be *hypothetical*, a posit, and not a first principle. And it would be *critical*, subject to ongoing refinement in light of new experience. Thus my title. It is a title I fancy Don would have liked, perhaps one he himself would have used had he ever taken up naturalism as a general theme.

It is much easier to give a negative characterization of naturalism than to provide a positive account of what it embraces. It is, of course, opposed to supernaturalism, particularly religious supernaturalism. In his most sustained autobiographical work (1981), Campbell reports that "by high school or early college, I had drifted away from whatever belief in God I had had as a child. . . ." And in his most well-known epistemological work ("Evolutionary Epistemology") he wrote: "We once 'saw' as through the fumblings of a blind protozoan, and no revelation has been given to us since." But naturalism also rejects the imposition of *a priori* principles whose justification would have to appeal to something beyond human experience. Again referring to the evolution of humans from protozoa, he wrote, "At no stage has there been any transfusion of knowledge from the outside, nor of mechanisms of knowing, nor of fundamental certainties." It is because of claims like these that we can be quite sure that Campbell was a naturalist, at least in the negative sense.

On the positive side, we can be sure Campbell would have insisted his naturalism be evolutionary. For his minimal position we can take the famous opening sentence of "Evolutionary Epistemology" with the word "naturalism" substituted for "epistemology": An evolutionary naturalism would be, at a minimum, a naturalism taking cognizance of and compatible with man's status as a product of evolution. This is a view no contemporary naturalist could reject. Campbell's own evolutionary epistemology, of course, went far beyond the minimal position. Besides being critical and hypothetical, however, it is not clear in what *other* ways his evolutionary naturalism would have gone beyond this minimum.

Here is my own suggestion for at least the form of a positive characterization of naturalism: Naturalism is the position that all aspects of the world can be given a naturalistic explanation. Scientific explanations are the obvious exemplars for naturalistic explanations, but I would not want to rule out historical explanations in the form of narratives expressed in every-day concepts, or, indeed, every-day explanations themselves, so long as they make no overt appeals to a transcendental realm.[1]

What, one might reasonably ask, constitutes a scientific explanation? The best general answer a naturalist can give is: A scientific explanation is an explanation sanctioned by a recognized science. To say more is to risk going beyond the bounds of naturalism. At the most general level, not being willing to appeal to essences, naturalists cannot attempt to solve the demarcation problem by providing a definition that separates science from non-science. At a less abstract level, naturalists know that what counts as a scientific explanation changes over time. For most of the seventeenth century, for example, mechanical explanations appealing to action at a distance would have been rejected. In the eighteenth century, after the impact of Newton's *Principia*, such explanations became commonplace. Ultimately, naturalists can do no more than follow such historical developments. This does not mean that naturalists cannot criticize scientific practices. Such criticism, however, can only be based on common sense or on a critical understanding of *other* scientific practices, there being no extra-scientific basis for any other sort of appeal.

The problem with the above positive characterization of naturalism is that it is very difficult to defend against the charge of simply begging the question against all those who would appeal to the supernatural, or, more likely, to *a priori* principles. How could anyone know that all aspects of reality have a scientific explanation? In the face of this question, the great danger is that the would-be naturalist will fall into the trap of trying to provide a transcendental argument for naturalism. That would be self-defeating. Here we can invoke Campbell's ideas and insist that naturalism be both critical and hypothetical. The possibility of a naturalistic explanation for everything must remain a hypothesis subject to critical examination. My own position is not so different.

My recommendation for naturalists would be to take a *methodological* turn. Characterize naturalism not as doctrine, but as method. A general formulation of the method would be something like this: For any aspect of the world, seek a naturalistic rather than a supernaturalistic explanation. It is a virtue of a methodological stance that its adoption does not require a transcendental justification. Commitment to the method can be somewhat justified by appeal to past successes at finding naturalistic explanations. One might even argue that the success rate has been going up for the past three hundred years. More than that one cannot do without going outside a naturalistic stance. I think would-be naturalists should settle for the methodological stance. But again, naturalists remain free to *criticize* non-naturalistic explanations as being unjustified, incoherent, vacuous, contradicting established science, and so on. One must only not pretend to an *a priori* refutation of non-naturalistic pretensions.

Naturalistic Priority

In order further to develop the above conception of naturalism, I will present and illustrate several more specific methodological maxims intended as additions to the general maxim stated above. The first of these I call "Naturalistic Priority." It is best illustrated by the historically most important exemplar for naturalistic explanations, Darwin's explanation of the origin of species.

The historical background to Darwin's theory included a strong tradition of natural theology in which the design of nature, particularly the design of animals and humans, was taken as evidence for a supernatural designer and creator. Darwin did not provide direct evidence *against* the existence of such a god. Rather, his theory of evolution by natural selection provided an *alternative, scientific* explanation of the acknowledged facts regarding the fit between the functional anatomy of animals and their environment. The arguments of natural theology were thereby undercut. The existing adaptation of organisms to their environments could be explained without recourse to a divine designer. Ordinary causal mechanisms producing variation, selection, and transmission of traits could do the job.[2]

The methodological principle I am calling "naturalistic priority" may be stated as follows: The availability of a *naturalistic* explanation of a recognized phenomenon renders unnecessary any non-naturalistic explanation. Obviously this principle is not neutral as between naturalistic and non-naturalistic explanations. It is not intended to be otherwise. It is part of a methodological strategy for developing a thoroughgoing naturalistic approach to an understanding of the world.

My statement of the principle of naturalistic priority makes reference to *available* scientific explanations. What makes a scientific explanation "available"? On the one hand, logical possibility is too weak an interpretation, for that makes application of the naturalistic strategy too easy. Presumably any phenomenon could logically be the result of the fortuitous coming together of natural causes. On the other hand, one cannot require a fully confirmed scientific hypothesis. Darwin's original theory of evolution was notoriously lacking a satisfactory account of inheritance, something essential to his account of evolution. Yet that did not prevent many serious-minded people from regarding it as a viable alternative to special creation. So an "available" scientific explanation must be one that, relative to the science accepted at the time, is plausible enough that something not too different is likely eventually to prove correct. This remains somewhat vague, but seems about as good as one can do.

Naturalistic Justification of Epistemological Norms

One of the standard objections leveled at naturalism is that it is powerless to deal with the *normative* elements of life. Indeed, it is often claimed that naturalism is powerless to account for the norms that underlie scientific practice itself. The basis for this objection is the assumption that science is only descriptive and that one cannot derive anything normative from something merely descriptive. Here we are on Campbell's home ground, descriptive epistemology.[3]

One must distinguish two kinds of norms, *categorical* and *conditional*. Categorical norms prescribe or proscribe various actions unconditionally. They simply say, "Do this" or "Do not do that." Conditional norms have the form: "If you want to achieve G, do A." It is true, I think, that, within a naturalistic framework, one cannot *justify* categorical norms. One can, however, *explain* them. Conditional norms, on the other hand, can be *justified* naturalistically, and science requires only conditional norms. When Campbell talked about the hypothetical normativity of evolutionary epistemology, he was appealing to conditional norms.

Before saying anything more about the epistemological norms of science, I must say something about my conception of the objects to which those norms apply. Much philosophy of science presupposes a framework in which the focus is on linguistic entities, statements, and in which the connection between statements and the world is understood in terms of the notions of reference and truth. For many reasons, which I will not develop here, I think these notions too crude a basis for a satisfactory understanding of science. A richer, more satisfactory, picture results from introducing intermediate representational entities, for which I use the designation "models." Models may be characterized using statements, but these function in this context merely as definitions. Models may also be characterized, often only partially, using *non*-linguistic means, such as diagrams or actual scale models.

On this view, the empirical representational relationship is not directly between statements and the world, but between models and the world. Here the operative notion is not truth, but similarity, or "fit," between a model and world. Of course one can formulate the hypothesis that the model fits the world and ask whether this hypothesis is true. But such uses of the concept of truth can be understood in a purely semantic, redundant fashion. To say it is true that the model fits is merely a meta-linguistic way of saying that the model fits. The former claim adds no empirical content not already contained in the latter.[4]

I realize full well that the required notion of similarity, or fit, requires further explication. Here one could follow Campbell (1974b) in invoking the evolutionary notion of the "fit" of organisms to their environment. Think of the operative part of a scientific theory as a population of specific models. The relationship of a theory fitting the world may then be thought of as being like the fit of a population of organisms to its environment. Individual models then fit the world in something like the way individual organisms fit their environment. This analogy at least makes it clear that the fit of individual models to the world is multidimensional and that the fit of an overall theory is ever changing and never perfect. It gets one away from thinking of theories in terms of the over-simple notions of reference and truth. I would not claim too much more for the analogy.

Returning to the problem of providing a naturalistic justification for epistemic norms, I will focus on the special case of a crucial experiment with two rival models. The experiment is assumed to have an observable output which, for purposes of illustration, we can represent schematically as a one dimensional range, R, of numerical values. The models and the experimental set-up should be related as follows:

(i) If the model M_1 provides a good fit to the real world, then it is very probable that the experiment will yield an outcome in the range R_1, and very improbable that it will yield an outcome in the range R_2.

(ii) If the model M_2 provides a good fit to the real world, then it is very probable that the experiment will yield an outcome in the range R_2 and very improbable that it will yield an outcome in the range R_1.

The decision rule is: If the set-up yields a reading in the range R_1, choose model M_1 as the best fitting model. If the set-up yields a reading in the range R_2, choose model M_2 as the best fitting model.

The conditional epistemological norm is: If one wishes to decide empirically which of two rival models better fits the world, design an experiment satisfying the conditions stated above. The justification for the usefulness of this norm is that an experiment satisfying these conditions provides a basis for a reliable decision between the two models. To see why this is so, one need only review the situation as presented above. Given the stated design features, if M_1 does provide a good fit to the world, it is very likely that one will observe a reading in the range R_1 and, correctly, choose M_1. Similarly if M_2 in fact best fits the world. In either case, one has a good chance of making the correct choice. Of course there is always the possibility that neither model fits the world very well and that the experiment yields a result in some intermediate range. In that case, the whole experiment is simply inconclusive.[5]

It is important to realize that the conditional norms for deciding which of two models best fits the world do not require any backing by *categorical* norms. We do not require a categorical norm such as: "Thou shalt decide which of two models best fits the world," or, more generally, "Thou shalt do science." There is no such categorical imperative. One always does science because of some other goals.[6]

I would not claim that this is the only way of understanding the epistemology of science that can be justified naturalistically. That there is one way is enough to show that a naturalized epistemology of science is possible. The only major possible philosophical objection to this explanation is that it is subject to a regress. That is, applying the principles of design requires substantive knowledge of the physical probabilities of the experimental set-up. If this knowledge were based on previous experiments, they would require similar assumptions, and so on. Pursuing this line of argument leads to a quest for a foundational inductive method that can be applied with no prior general knowledge whatsoever and whose use can be justified *a priori*. I do not think that such a quest could be successful.[7] Neither did Campbell.

Evolutionary Change in Science

It will have been noted that there is nothing particularly evolutionary about my understanding of that part of scientific epistemology concerned with the empirical testing of scientific hypotheses. This is not to deny, as Campbell insisted, that these ideas about testing hypotheses are not themselves the product of social evolution. What may be more directly evolutionary, on my view, is not so much the strict epistemology of science as the nature of historical change in science.

Here, as in Darwin's time, the primary alternative is a teleological view of science—science as progressing by accumulating ever more comprehensive and ever more detailed truths about the world. The goal is the whole truth about the universe.

Kuhn's *Structure of Scientific Revolutions* (1962) provided the major challenge of this century to the teleological picture of science. Numerous historical and sociological studies have since confirmed the importance of historical contingencies for producing all sorts of changes in science—some small, some large. It is useful, in a modest way, to organize these historical contingencies into an evolutionary pattern of variation, selection, and transmission.

Most evolutionary accounts of science, such as Toulmin's (1972), emphasize the evolution of *conceptual* objects such as theories. I would put the focus elsewhere, namely, on the evolution of research groups within research specialties. The models with which individual scientists are committed can then be seen as *traits* of the individuals. The relative distribution of these traits within the research group evolves over time. The central issue is: What are the *mechanisms* underlying the variation, selection, and transmission of these intellectual traits within research groups? Most of these mechanisms, I think, are *cognitive* or *social*. It is thus cognitive and social mechanisms which determine whether any particular research group grows or declines in importance within a research specialty. This point of view seems to me in keeping with Campbell's conception of "science's social system of validity-enhancing collective belief change" (1986) and his insistence that descriptive epistemology be psychological and sociological as well as evolutionary.[8]

If one wishes to maintain any sort of realist view of science, *one* of these mechanisms must be the outcomes of experimental tests of various models. Individuals must be differentially motivated to switch their allegiance from one sort of model to another as a result of experimental outcomes. Similarly, the experimental success of some types of models must provide a positive motivation for new recruits into the general area to join the corresponding research group. Experimental success, however, remains but one mechanism relevant to the differential growth of one research group over others. Access to material resources to support graduate and post-graduate students is also an important mechanism. So is the participation of inspiring teachers and enterprising academic organizers.[9]

In sum, applying an evolutionary model to the changes that take place in scientific fields provides a good way of organizing our understanding science, a far better way than provided by the old teleological model. But the evolutionary model, by itself, provides little basis for understanding the details of any changes in science. For that one must look at the *mechanisms* operative in the processes of variation, selection, and transmission. And these mechanisms are, by and large, not biological, but cognitive and social. So evolutionary models provide only a part of our total picture of science. To invoke a biological analogy, the cognitive and social mechanisms provide the genetics for an evolutionary model of science. Just as evolutionary theory was incomplete until the synthesis with genetics in the twentieth century, so any evolutionary model of science will remain incomplete until it incorporates appropriate cognitive and social models.

The Problem of Realism

I want now to focus on the problem of scientific realism as it arises even for the modestly evolutionary picture of science outlined above. The problem is this. According to this evolutionary picture, the course of science is highly contingent on accidents of history. So the models of the world held at any given time might have been quite different if historical contingencies had been different. On the other hand, the truths about the world are commonly regarded as being fixed. So what reason could there be for thinking that what we have now are truths since we could have just as well now held different models of the world? Similarly, with all the contingencies built into the evolutionary development of science, what reason could we have for thinking that we are, over time, getting *closer* to the truth? So even a modestly evolutionary picture of science seems incompatible with scientific realism.

My solution to this problem is to keep the evolutionary picture of science and revise the conception of scientific realism. In fact, the standard conception of scientific realism is largely a carry-over from the old teleological picture of science. It is time it be revised in any case. The clearest expression of the old picture is to be found in those areas of philosophy least familiar to people outside of philosophy—the philosophy of mathematics and logic, and formal semantics. The idea is that the structure of reality mirrors the structure of set theory. Reality is conceived of as consisting of discrete objects, sets of discrete objects, sets of sets of objects, sets of ordered pairs of objects, and so on. True statements are those that describe objects as belonging to the sets to which they in fact belong. A complete science would consist of all and only the true statements about this set-theoretical reality.

This scheme works quite well for understanding purely mathematical entities where only abstract structure matters and empirical meaningfulness not at all. The assumption among philosophers of science for most of this century has been that the same sort of scheme must work for empirical science as well. The tacit argument seems to have been that physics is the fundamental science, and physics is highly mathematical, so our understanding of notions of reference and truth developed for mathematics must work also for physics, and, by implication, for all of science. One need only openly state this argument to realize that this picture of science is not necessarily correct.

Here is an alternative picture. Imagine the universe as having a definite structure, but exceedingly complex, so complex that no models humans can devise could capture more than limited aspects of the total complexity. Nevertheless, some ways of constructing models of the world do provide resources for capturing some aspects of the world more or less well. Other ways may provide resources for capturing other aspects more or less well. Both ways, however, may capture some aspects of reality and thus be candidates for a realistic understanding of the world. So here, in principle, is a solution to the problem of finding a picture of science that is both evolutionary and realistic. It does not matter that different evolutionary paths might lead to different sciences. Each might genuinely capture some aspects of reality.

This way of presenting the alternative picture makes it seem like a piece of *a priori* metaphysics, something no naturalist can allow. The same picture can, however, be presented as a methodological precept: Proceed as if the world were this way. As such it needs no *a priori* justification. Its vindication would be in its success. I believe that many scientists tacitly operate successfully with just such a methodological stance. This is difficult to prove, however, because their explicit rhetoric tends to reflect the traditional teleological picture codified by philosophers.

I suggest the term "perspective" to designate a way of constructing scientific models. Within a perspective, some models may be discovered experimentally to fit the world better than others, at least for some purposes. Comparisons across perspectives are more difficult, but I doubt one ever finds the kind of radical incommensurability that philosophers such as Kuhn and Feyerabend are supposed to have advocated. In any case, the resulting view of realism can be called "perspectival realism." I will give some examples shortly. My main task now is to make plausible a realistic understanding of science that is perspectival rather than absolute.[10]

Perspectivism in Observation

Perspectivism is most easily appreciated at the level of observation. It is here that the metaphor of perspectives is closest to its roots. The evolutionary development of perceptual mechanisms and their role in knowledge acquisition was a persistent theme in Campbell's writings.[11]

A paradigm example would be the experience of viewing a building from different angles and different distances. Each distance and angle of view provides a different perspective on the building. Two features of this simple case already exemplify the main features of a more general perspectivism. First, there is no total or universal perspective, or, alternatively, there is no perspective from nowhere or from everywhere at once. All perspectives are partial, relative to their objects. Second, each perspective is a perspective of the building. There is something real that each perspective is a perspective of. So perspectivism is *prima facie* a form of realism, not constructivism. Additional objectivity can be built into this example by imagining a series of photographs taken from different viewpoints rather than simply a series of visual experiences.

The example of secondary qualities stretches the metaphor of perspectivism a bit further. We perceive the world as containing objects exhibiting different colors. Yet we know it is our capacity for experiencing color that partly explains the character of our perceptions. Without perceivers like us, there would be no experiences of color. Nevertheless, our perception of color provides us access to aspects of the world apart from us, namely differential reflection of light waves of varying frequency. I would say that our capacity for color vision provides us with a perspective from which we can experience aspects of the world. It is again not an excessive extension of the metaphor to say that different species of animals experience the world from the different perspectives provided by their various sense organs.[12]

The existence of scientific instrumentation provides a further extension of the metaphor. Radio telescopes, for example, may be said to provide us with a perspective from which to view the heavens. It is a different perspective from that provided by more ordinary optical telescopes. Without this new technology, the kinds of outputs provided by such instruments would not exist. Yet radio telescopes do provide us with information about aspects of the universe that may not be accessible in other ways. Similar comments apply to the gamma ray telescopes that provided the evidence for reports of a plume of antimatter (positrons) streaming out from the center of our galaxy.[13]

These paradigm examples suggest that all forms of observation and/or detection should be understood as perspectival in nature. They all provide access to aspects of reality, access that is nevertheless always partial.

Perspectivism in Theories

The extension of perspectivism to the level of scientific theory is more problematic, but, I think, eventually equally convincing.

As an intermediate step, consider the human practice of making *maps*. Maps, I would say, represent spatial regions from particular perspectives determined by various human interests. Imagine, for example, four different maps of Manhattan Island (New York City): (1) a street map; (2) a subway map; (3) a neighborhood map; and (4) a geological map. Each, I claim, represents the island of Manhattan from a different perspective utilized, respectively, by a driver, a subway rider, a social worker, a geologist.

Maps exhibit the two primary characteristics I earlier ascribed to perspectives. First, they are always *partial*. There is no such thing as a complete map. Second, maps may be maps *of something*. So maps can be understood realistically. Unlike perceptual experience or the operation of physical detectors, however, the production of a map is an act of deliberate construction. If a nervous system or other physical detector is functioning properly, it automatically registers the information available to it from its particular perspective. Insuring that a map correctly represents the intended space requires much deliberate care. Mistakes can easily be made. Moreover, one can deliberately construct mistaken maps, or even maps of completely fictional places.

One is tempted to ask: How do maps represent physical spaces? Asking the question this way suggests that the answer is to be found in some binary relationship between maps and places. A better question is: How do we humans manage to use maps to represent physical spaces? This way of posing the question makes it less easy to forget that making maps is a cognitive and social activity of humans.

Part of the answer is that map-making and map-using takes advantage of similarities in spatial structure between features of a map and features of a terrain. But one cannot understand map-making solely in terms of abstract, geometrical relationships. Interpretative relationships are also necessary. One must be able to understand that a particular area on a map is intended to represent, for example, a neighborhood rather than a political division or corporate ownership. These two features of representation using maps, similarity of structure and interpretation, carry over to an understanding of how humans use scientific models to represent aspects of the world.

It is again not too great an analogical leap, I think, to go from maps to the kinds of models one finds in many sciences. Classical mechanics provides an archetypal example. The models of classical mechanics represent only a very limited number of aspects of objects such as mass, position, velocity, and acceleration. This being so, I would say that the principles of classical mechanics provide a perspective within which one can construct a wide variety of models, some of which we have found to provide a very good fit to mechanical systems in the real world.

Consider, for example, textbook representations of a simple harmonic oscillator. These typically contain numerous equations used to characterize the model. But they also often include a number of diagrams which look a lot like maps. That is, these diagrams are made up of lines in two dimensions which represent various aspects of the motion of a simple harmonic oscillator. One need only know how to interpret them.

Here, then, is a suggestion for better understanding what it means for a model to fit the world. The fit between a model and the world may be thought of like the fit between a map and the region it represents. How further to understand that sort of fit is, unfortunately, not obvious.

One World as a Methodological Rule

A final problem. Suppose we have two perspectives that overlap, but disagree about the character of the world in the region where they overlap. What should we say? We might try to brush off the question with the reflection that, since we are only concerned with applying models, what does it matter if applications conflict? Use the type of model that best serves one's current purposes. I find that attitude understandable, but too instrumentalistic.

The basis for my misgiving is the supposition that there is, after all, only one world, and it has some one structure or other. Of course, from a naturalistic perspective, one cannot offer transcendental arguments in favor of a "one world" hypothesis. One can, however, take it as a methodological rule: Proceed as if the world has a single structure. In light of this rule, the existence of conflicting applications of different types of models is an indication that one or both types of models fail to fit the world as well as they might. It is an invitation to further inquiry to find models that eliminate the conflict, although there is no guarantee that such models will be found. If arguments in favor of adopting this methodological rule are desired, the best one can do is point out the many cases in the history of science where following such a rule was fruitful in leading to the construction of better models. The eventual resolution of the early twentieth century conflict between Mendelians and biometricians seems to me a clear case in point.

Conclusion

I conclude that naturalism is a viable general project, capable of encompassing all of nature, including culture and the enterprise of science itself. The role of evolutionary thinking within a naturalist program is a matter for continued investigation. It cannot, I think, be all encompassing in a useful way. As Campbell insisted regarding descriptive epistemology, it must be cognitive and social as well as evolutionary.

One must be careful, however, how one characterizes naturalism. Presented as theses, it invites requests for justification and self-defeating attempts to construct transcendental arguments in its favor. Vigilance is required to keep arguments for naturalism within naturalistic limitations. A better strategy, I have suggested, is to regard naturalism as a set of methodological rules for developing a consistent naturalistic picture of the world. Success in applying these rules gives comfort to those pursuing the program and encourages others to join the effort. Positively, that is the most a consistent naturalist can do. I feel confident that Campbell would have been happy to embrace such a critical hypothetical evolutionary naturalism.

Notes

1. This characterization assumes that scientific theories themselves do not embody *a priori* claims.

2. Historians of science debate just how deep Darwin's own commitment to this form of argument might have been. There is no doubt that later thinkers regarded the argument as I have here presented it. See, for example, Chapter 3 of William James's famous lectures on Pragmatism (1907).

3. "Descriptive Epistemology: Psychological, Sociological, and Evolutionary" was the title of Campbell's famous 1977 William James Lectures, now finally published in (Campbell 1988e), with the exception of Lecture 2, which appeared as (Campbell 1987a). Twenty years later these lectures still stand out as very timely and worthy of publication on their own.

4. The above two paragraphs are a very hasty summary of the view presented in chap. 3 of (Giere 1988) and in (Giere 1995, 1999).

5. The above argument is elaborated in (Giere 1983) and chap. 6 of (Giere 1988).

6. For an exchange on the issue of whether scientific epistemology requires categorical norms, see (Siegel 1989) and my reply (Giere 1989).

7. The only attempt I know that even comes close to satisfying these conditions is Reichenbach's (1949, chap. 11) famous pragmatic justification of induction, and even it, as Ian Hacking (1968) proved, does not work.

8. I have developed these ideas in greater detail in (Giere 1990).

9. Campbell's poignant study (1979b) of the different leadership styles of Edward Tolman and Kenneth Spence is relevant here.

10. Several years ago, Don Campbell read a draft paper of mine outlining the basic idea of perspectival realism. He liked the idea and sent me some valuable materials on the history of perspectivalism. That act was typical of his generosity toward many people in the profession.

11. See, for example, (Campbell 1974b; 1988e, Part 5).

12. This simply states in perspectival terms a point Campbell made often, though never developed in great detail.

13. My point here is more general than simply claiming that every instrument has a finite bandwidth. It is that there are indeterminately many different instruments which detect different kinds of signals.

5

On Being a Philosophical Naturalist: A Tribute to Donald Campbell

MICHAEL RUSE

To know Don Campbell was to love him. He bubbled over with warmth and enthusiasm for people and for ideas. I well remember my first meeting with him some twenty years ago when he was at Syracuse University. I was visiting the philosophy department, but he had heard that I was coming and asked to see me. I sat in his office for an hour while he grilled me in a searching manner, trying to find out my beliefs and probing their weaknesses: not at all in a spirit of antagonism, but simply trying to learn from others and to see where his own thinking could be improved or extended. There was absolutely no pretending that he was in some sense superior (of course it would have been no pretense in the relationship between him and me). He wanted to reach out and to ask one to share with him the excitement of ideas and the exploration of the intellectually unknown. There are some people that one feels privileged to call a friend, and Don Campbell was one of those.

I do not know how much Campbell influenced me over the years, as I (like so many others) made a move towards a naturalistic philosophy. I do know that I have taken as my personal motto Campbell's (1977) humorous comments at the beginning of his William James Lectures: enterprises such as engaged persons like us require a willingness to be inadequate in many fields at once! I myself have tried to articulate a personal philosophy, both of epistemology and of ethics, taking seriously Darwinian evolutionary theory. Campbell's influence has been profound, even when—perhaps especially when—our ways have parted (especially important was Campbell, 1974b). Here, in tribute to Don Campbell, I do not intend simply to recover old ground. Rather, I shall share with you some of my thinking over the past decade as I have tried to extend my naturalistic philosophy into thinking about problems about the nature of science. I do not know if Don would agree with the conclusions that I draw, but I am sure that he would empathize with the kind of enterprise in which I have been engaged.

The Problem of Values

One of the biggest debates today engaging those interested in the nature of science is about ultimate questions. Is science in some sense objective, a reflection of disinterested reality? Or is science, rather, subjective, a epiphenomenon of either individual ideas or cultural norms: practices, expectations, and aspirations? Is science, as the late Sir Karl Popper (1959, 1972) used to say, "knowledge without a knower"? Or is it rather a "social construction"? That is to say, is it something on a par with religion, philosophy, or literary studies: a mere pimple on the cultural backside of the day (Collins 1985; Shapin and Schaffer 1985; Young 1985)?

The traditional philosophical way of attempting to resolve such a dispute as this is through *a priori* methods: linguistic analyses, for instance. One tries to discover the meanings of words and the ways in which they are used and so forth. One analyzes the concepts involved and sees if they are consistent and the like. What one does not do is turn to the real world in search of answers. Indeed, such a turn is considered not merely unnecessary but slightly vulgar, philosophically speaking. The real task of the philosopher is taken to be that of trying through conceptual analysis to arrive at the truth, and from there of making prescriptions about what scientists do or should not do in a world of perfect rationality.

The naturalistic approach, to the contrary, feels that appeal absolutely must be made to the real world (Callebaut, 1994; Hull, 1988a; Ruse, 1986). It starts by looking around at the best body of knowledge that humans have managed to achieve and—for all its faults—finds this in science. Particularly in the period since the Scientific Revolution, the enterprise of science has built up a staggeringly impressive edifice. Most other areas, to the contrary—religion for instance, or philosophy—have lagged far behind. In the case of religion, indeed, one might say that it has seen precipitous decline since the Scientific Revolution. Hence, the philosophical naturalist argues that the way to do philosophy, and to revitalize it, is to try as much as possible to adopt the techniques and practices of the physical scientist. One is not a physical scientist as such, but one is going to model one's practice on such a person.

What does this mean in the case of something like the philosophy of biology? The biologist, that is, the student of the life sciences, takes organisms as his or her subject matter. If, for instance, he or she is a physiologist, then the aim is to study the workings of the body: one looks at such questions as how it is that the organism functions at the levels of nerves and muscles, and what biochemical reactions are involved in keeping a body at a constant temperature. The evolutionary biologist likewise studies organisms, although perhaps not just the individual but large numbers of animals or plants spread over space and time. One is interested in the interactions between different organisms, both within and without the species, as well as the ways in which organisms change according to varying needs and circumstances.

The philosopher of biology *qua* philosopher has no direct interest in organisms. Rather such a person is interested in the products of the scientist: the theories, hypotheses, concepts, ideas and the like, that the practicing biologist has produced, both in our age and in the past. Hence, what the philosopher of biology (as a naturalist) is trying to do is to apply the methods of the biologist—the methods of other scientists, for that matter—not to organisms, but to biologists-thinking-about-organisms. In other words, what I suggest is that as a naturalist interested in a major philosophical question about the nature of science—Is it objective or subjective?—I should use as my data the products of the working biologists, as the working biologists in turn use as their data the activities and nature of organisms. (There is some danger of circularity here. If one is to try to understand the science, is it legitimate to use the science itself as an aid to this understanding? I see no escape from this problem. In a sense, obviously one is engaged in a circular enterprise. However, I would suggest that it is not a viciously circular process, but rather one of those common situations in which, as it were, one is trying to deepen the depth of one's understanding as one appeals to ideas and then gets feedback and so forth. One may never get out of the loop in one sense, but one gets ever-greater insight into what we can truly know. Taking an attitude like this, although I admit that this is surely a matter which requires further study, immodestly I offer the fruits of my inquiry as proof of the worth of the naturalistic approach. One can always stop circularity by assuming certain propositions *a priori*, but I am not sure that that is much of a solution.)

How is one to move from a general approach to a specific inquiry? How is one to take the commitment to naturalism and apply it to the question of the objectivity and subjectivity of science, of biology in particular? To use an ugly but useful term, one needs some way of operationalizing the issue. I am sufficiently in accord with Charles Darwin himself to think that simply going into the field, as it were, and looking for answers will not do. Unless one goes looking with some ideas or suggestions already at least partially formulated, one will get nowhere: even though one may well want to revise or reject one's initial ideas before one has finished. In other words, one wants some way of being able to generate hypotheses which one can then go out and test. Which all means that one wants some area or areas where one can focus one's attention. Simply trying to consider the whole of the history of biology, at one time, would be as futile as trying to consider the whole flora and fauna of Canada at one time. Every working biologist knows full well that finding the right organism for the right question is a crucial part of the scientific enterprise. No less for the naturalist engaged in philosophical inquiry. Finding the right topic to discuss, hoping thereby to answer some questions, is an absolutely crucial part of the naturalistic philosophical enterprise.

Let us take a leaf out of the books of conventional philosophers of science. As far as the matter of operationalizing our discussion specifically about objectivity and subjectivity, I would argue that concentrating on the question of values will prove very profitable (McMullin, 1983). On the one hand, we have those values which are presumed to promote the ultimate value of the objectivist: truth. One has those values which help one to put one's ideas or theories in true correspondence with a disinterested external reality. These values are often known as "epistemic values": they include such things being able to make strong and well-confirmed predictions; being consistent with other theories and coherent within one's own work; and aiming for a kind of unification, what William Whewell (1840) termed a "consilience of inductions" in which one gathers together many different ideas under a single hypothesis. Also important is being fertile in the sense of showing new directions of work and ways in which one can make new kinds of predictions, and—to round out the list, albeit with something somewhat more troublesome in the eyes of many—there is the epistemic virtue of showing a certain simplicity or elegance. Again and again, one finds scientists feeling certain that hypotheses must be true because they simply are too beautiful or too elegant to be false.

On the other hand, when one thinks of the case made by the subjectivists, or social constructivists, one finds again and again that they emphasize the cultural, the non-epistemic, value-laden nature of the scientific enterprise. This group of people argues that science reflects all sorts of social and cultural values: religious values, for instance, racial values, sexual values (both in comparing one sex as opposed to another and one sexual orientation as opposed to another), political values, and much, much more. It is argued by the constructivists that scientific theories often adopt a facade of objectivity, but in fact they are simply vehicles for promoting the ideals and commitments of people who produce the science (Longino, 1990).

The question for the naturalist, then, is that of checking the history of biology against claims about epistemic values as opposed to claims about non-epistemic or cultural values. But which part of the history of biology should one choose? Given my own background and expertise, I fall naturally on the area of the history of evolutionary biology. This is certainly a fair choice because in recent years the subjectivists, in particular, have held evolutionary biology up for analysis, finding it to be absolutely loaded with cultural values. Usually cultural values of a particularly undesirable kind. It is thought to be racist, sexist, politically unacceptable, and a great deal more (Lewontin, 1991; Hubbard, 1983; Gould, 1981; Rose, 1998). In choosing an area like evolutionary biology, if we come out with conclusions which are less than a hundred percent sympathetic to the subjectivists, no one can accuse of having slanted the discussion by the judicious choice of an atypical case study.

Hypotheses about Progress

As I have just said, all sorts of non-epistemic values are supposedly ingrained in evolutionary biology. I am going to focus on something which I myself have been studying intensely for the past ten years: the social or cultural idea of progress (Ruse 1993, 1996). This is the idea that in some way, through effort unaided by any supernatural intervention, we humans can increase and improve our body of knowledge, our social state, our cultural systems, and much, much more. As a historian, I have been trying to see how this idea—undoubtedly cultural and value-impregnated through and through—has interacted with the idea of biological evolution ever since the middle of the eighteenth century when first people began to think seriously in terms of organic transformation. What I intend to do here, therefore, turning now to philosophy, is to rely on this Enlightenment idea—something which I found to impinge deeply with science—as my specific instance of a cultural value. I shall use it as my empirical datum or case study. My questions, therefore, will be directed to the interaction of the cultural value of progress with the biological theory of organic evolution.

What hypotheses might one generate in order to start one's inquiry? There are at least four scenarios that one might have expected to have found played out and these would reflect themselves into one's conclusions about the interactions of science and values, with consequent implications for the issue of scientific objectivity/subjectivity. Let me cast them in terms of hypotheses:

H 1.

The first hypothesis is that of the strict or traditional objectivist. This, I suspect, is the position that many practicing scientists would take (Perutz, 1995; Gross and Levitt, 1994; Weinberg, 1992). This hypothesis would expect to find that cultural values persist little or not at all in science. The epistemic is everything. It is true that perhaps cultural values might play some role in the formulation of the ideas of science—the context of discovery—but once the science gets cracking—the context of justification—they fall away. In my specific case, I presume one's hypothesis with respect to progress and evolutionary biology would be that, although progress could have had a hand in the initial conceiving of evolutionary ideas, it would last but a fleeting moment and be irrelevant from then on.

H 2.

Here we have the complete opposite to the objectivist. We have the extreme social constructivist position (Latour and Woolgar, 1979). This hypothesis suggests that social or cultural values persist indefinitely in scientific theories. Cast in terms of our case study, one would therefore expect to find that the cultural idea of progress was important in the initial conceiving of evolutionary ideas and that this value has persisted right down to the present. Evolutionary biology today, therefore, would be seen as a vehicle for social or cultural ideas: aspirations about ongoing, upward, human-fueled change.

H 3.

Here one would have some sort of modification of the first hypothesis. One would expect cultural values to be important in the initial stages of a scientific theory, but as the science matures, perhaps becomes more professionalized, one would expect to see the cultural values vanish (McMullin, 1983). What especially one might expect to find is that, down through time, epistemic virtues or values start to become more and more important in the scientific practitioner's thinking, and that as the epistemic rises it pushes the cultural to one side and eventually right out. Cast in terms of our case study, therefore, one might well expect to find that progress was very important in the initial conceiving of evolutionary ideas and that it persisted down through time. However, as evolutionary theory has matured one would find that epistemic factors like predictive accuracy, and unificatory power and fertility, become more and more significant. With this change, cultural values including progress get diminished or excluded.

H 4.

This hypothesis is a variant on the constructivist hypothesis. Here one would assume that cultural values will stay within science, but one would recognize that as culture changes so do the values within it. Hence, one might expect to find the science itself reflecting these changes. In other words, one would expect to find scientific change, but fueled less by epistemic factors and more by cultural factors. In the terms of our study, one would therefore expect to find perhaps that peoples' attitudes towards progress as a cultural notion change, and that this reflects in the evolutionary biology (Wagar, 1972). Today's evolutionary biology might be just as value-impregnated as it was in the eighteenth century: it is just that the cultural values have changed.

Here then we have four hypotheses. I should say that many philosophically sophisticated people today would endorse some version of H 3 (hypothesis number three). Trying to steer a course between extreme objectivity and no less extreme subjectivity, they would think that perhaps science begins in subjectivity, but through the decades—through the centuries perhaps—matures into an objective science. In fact, evolutionary biology is often taken to be an exemplar of precisely this philosophy (Hesse and Arbib, 1986). Initially the science was indeed deeply progress-impregnated: but then two events occurred, both of which promote the epistemic, and both of which push progress to one side and eventually right out of the science. First, some hundred years after the first evolutionists, Charles Darwin published his *On The Origin of Species* (1859). His chief mechanism is that of natural selection, but this is (as everyone knows) a relativistic mechanism in the sense that those that survive at any particular time are those that have the needed features for survival at that time, and the fittest are defined in terms of survival. What counts as fitness in one situation at some time and place is not necessarily what proves fitness in another situation at another time or place. There is therefore no absolute up or down, just a question of what works in the circumstances. Camouflage against a white background is white; camouflage against a black background is black. This being so, there is no hope of any kind of absolute progress, because everything is relativized.

Then, some fifty years or so after Darwin came the forerunner of today's theory of heredity, so-called Mendelian genetics. This was important for evolutionary theory because it provided the raw blocks from which evolutionary change is built. But, as is well known, it is an absolutely essential part of Mendelian genetics that the new variations in populations, caused by so-called mutations in the genes, are random—random not in the sense of being uncaused, but in the sense of appearing without any connection to the needs of their possessors. In fact, most mutations are deleterious. Once again, therefore, we have a factor which is making progress seem less and less plausible. Although, let it also be noted, Mendelian genetics no less than Darwinian selection, was embraced by evolutionists for its epistemic virtues. Hence, we have a perfect exemplar of hypothesis three at work.

I should perhaps say that I myself, before I began on my case study, rather favored H 4. This essentially is a revision of the social constructivist hypothesis (H 2). But here we argue that although cultural values do persist in science, there is absolutely no reason why such values themselves should not change. Indeed, we suspect that over the course of one or two centuries cultural values might be expected to change. In other words, one expects to find that the science changes, but that it changes less as a function of epistemic factors and more as a function of changing social mores. In the case of evolution and progress, what this might mean is that although evolutionary theory was impregnated at some point with progressivist ideas, this is no longer the case. Hence, here we find a change in evolutionism itself. I favored this hypothesis because it is no secret that today many intellectuals, particularly in the West, are very dubious about social progress (in strong contradistinction to their grandparents and other forefathers) (Bury, 1920; Almond et al., 1982). This is an age of world wars, of nuclear weapons, of global warming, and of horrendous worldwide diseases like AIDS: who truly can speak of progress? Or so many people today wonder. My suspicion was that one would find this changing attitude towards cultural progress reflected in evolutionary thinking: the reason why we might not expect to find progressivism in today's evolutionary writings is not so much because cultural values have gone, but because the values have changed.

My personal inclinations to one side, we have now before us four hypotheses. Of course, any practicing scientist will tell you that there are always an infinite number of possible hypotheses, and one must be prepared to change and modify as one works along. So there is always the prospect that all four of these hypotheses will be shown false and a fifth (H 5) will appear as a more true reflection of what actually occurred. But this is just a reservation, one that can be discussed only after we have completed our work. And so, without further ado, let us turn to the case study.

The History of Evolutionary Thought

Evolutionary thought, like progress, is a child of the Enlightenment. One finds that it is around the middle of the eighteenth century that people start to make the first speculations about a natural origin of organisms, from a developmental perspective. By the end of the century, there were thinkers in several of the countries of Western Europe looking favorably on possible transformist origins, not only of life as we see it around us today, but also of life of the past as was being increasingly, rapidly revealed by geological explorations. This means that, counting back from today, we have roughly 250 years of history to consider. My findings are that one can appropriately divide this history into three parts. First, from 1750 to 1859, the year that Charles Darwin published his *On The Origin of Species*; then from 1859 to about 1940, the latter time being that when the so-called "synthetic theorists" put together modern evolutionary theory; then third, from 1940 to the present. Let me take these three periods in turn. (I will be brief. I have dealt with these matters elsewhere, especially in my *Monad to Man: The Concept of Progress in Evolutionary Biology* (1996) and my *Mystery of Mysteries: Is Evolution a Social Construction?* (1999). In those volumes, to use an ironic comment of David Hull, you will find all you need to know on the subject, and much, much more.)

Prominent figures in the early part of my first period are Erasmus Darwin (1791, 1789, 1794–96), the English physician and poet, friend of industrialists and grandfather of Charles Darwin, and Jean Baptiste de Lamarck, the French botanist and taxonomist, and author in 1809 of the first major evolutionary work, his *Philosophie zoologique* (1809). My claim is that, although both of these men were professionally qualified and respected in their own spheres, Darwin as a physician and Lamarck as a botanist, when it came to evolution their work was (with some justification) considered to be little more than speculation of a rather wild kind (McNeill, 1987; Burkhardt, 1977). Neither man allowed his theorizing to be constrained by sober obedience to epistemic constraints, nor did either attempt a rigorous survey of known empirical facts. Each, rather, preferred to glance at a wide range of phenomena, ranging from the reasonably sensible (like anatomical similarities) to the totally ludicrous (like reports from antiquity about the use of artificial phalluses to determine the sex of offspring). Their work, in other words, was loose and flabby and speculative—and was taken so by their contemporaries. It was certainly not considered to be something at the level of genuine science like physics and chemistry. It was rather regarded as more of a pseudoscience: very much at one with other pseudosciences of the day, notably mesmerism, the belief that there is a kind of animal magnetism which possesses people and which is responsible for all physical ailments. Respectable scientists of the day, notably the great French comparative anatomist Georges Cuvier (1813), were absolutely scathing about all such pseudosciences, and evolutionism in particular. In their opinion it was simply not the sort of thing that a reputable scientist produces.

This was the beginning. In fact, during the whole of the first period, virtually right up to the point when Darwin published, evolutionism stayed at this same low level. Probably the most significant evolutionary work published after Lamarck's *Philosophie zoologique*—certainly the one which gained the widest readership—was that published anonymously by the Scottish publisher, Robert Chambers: *Vestiges of the Natural History of Creation* (1844). This work was a hodgepodge of ideas, facts, speculations, half-truths, theological musings, and more. It was about as far from regular science, that is to say the kind of science then being produced by physicists and chemists and increasingly by students of the life sciences, as it is possible to imagine. Excoriated by respectable thinkers of all stripes, the evolutionism of *Vestiges* was considered to be no more genuine science than had been the evolutionism of Chambers's predecessors. The paradigm pseudoscience of the mid-nineteenth century was phrenology, the belief that there is a kind of science of brain bumps and that one's character can be inferred by the shape of one's head. It is significant and telling to learn that Chambers, in fact, set out to write a book on phrenology and for some reason halfway through changed his mind and ended by writing a book on evolution. One pseudoscience led smoothly to another!

This is not to say that by mid-century evolution was an unpopular idea. In fact, the pseudosciences frequently gain great popularity. I think today of the extent to which people consult astrological tables. *Vestiges* gained incredible popularity and was certainly read widely by many—indeed, it had significant influence, not the least on the work which gained Alfred Tennyson the poet laureateship (*In Memoriam*). After Chambers, particularly noteworthy (as the nineteenth century entered its second half) was the English social scientist and enthusiast for evolution, Herbert Spencer (Spencer, 1852a, b; 1857). He began to write at length—at very great length—on all sorts of matters including evolution. But although he was starting to spread the message far and wide, it is fair to say that even he was not able to do significant work in the direction of dragging evolutionism from the mire of pseudoscience.

All of that changes as we enter our second period in 1859. Charles Darwin's *On The Origin of Species* truly was a watershed event. He changed—it seems no exaggeration to say, he upgraded significantly—the status of evolutionary thinking. This was because of two things. First, Darwin provided a full and convincing argument for the very fact of evolutionary change. He did this by appealing to a unificatory or consilient type of argument (which incidentally he had learned from the philosopher-scientist William Whewell [1840]). He showed that, if one assumes evolution, then one can explain facts right across the biological board. Why for instance, it is that the finches of the Galápagos are very similar, but slightly different, and then again similar but different from the finches of the South African mainland? Why, for instance, it is that if we look at the fossil record we see a branching tree, roughly progressive from the simpler forms very different from those alive today? Why, for instance, it is that embryos of organisms very different as adults are significantly alike at the embryonic level? Why, for instance, it is that we see the isomorphisms, or homologies, between the bodies of organisms, even though the parts serve very different ends or functions? All of these questions, and many more, can be given a simple and straight answer if one assumes descent from common origins. Conversely, argued Darwin, descent from common origins is made probable—to the point of overwhelming likelihood—by the convergence of all of these different parts of biology.

Then, second, Darwin provided a mechanism for evolutionary change. He argued that more organisms are born than can possibly survive and reproduce, and that there is therefore a constant struggle for space, for food, and, above all, for mates. Together with this struggle for existence, Darwin noted that there is widespread variation always appearing in populations of wild organisms. He concluded, therefore, that those organisms which do survive and reproduce will, on average, be different from those that do not, and this success in the struggle will itself be a function (on average) of the differences between the successful (the fit) and the unsuccessful (the unfit). There will consequently, argued Darwin, be a natural form of selection. Given enough time, this will lead to full-blown evolution: evolution moreover of a particular kind, where organisms are adaptively fashioned towards their reproductive success. In other words, organisms will not be simply thrown together, but will be complex functioning wholes.

It was clearly Darwin's intention to upgrade evolutionary thinking from the pseudoscientific level in which it had been stuck for the previous century. I believe that he hoped to lay the foundation for a fully functioning, mature, professional science: a science of the same social level and epistemic quality as in areas of science like physics and chemistry. He hoped that evolution through natural selection would take its place alongside Newtonian mechanics and the atomic theory of contemporary chemistry. However, this was not to be, and for the whole of the second period of evolution's history, that is from 1859 to around 1940, it failed to achieve a fully mature professional status. Thanks to Darwin, it was no longer a pseudoscience, and indeed became part of the background thinking of all intellectuals in the West (and, as scholars are now showing increasingly, of intellectuals elsewhere in the world). No one, other than religious fanatics—particularly those found in the southern states of the U.S.—wanted to deny evolution as such, or even that evolution extends up to and includes our own species. However, although one might say evolution achieved the level of a popular science—it was an idea of the day in the late nineteenth century as it is in the late twentieth century—it failed to move all the way up the chain to the levels of physics and chemistry. For instance, very few wanted to make of evolution an experimental science: rather they preferred to use it as a kind of *Weltanschauung,* a kind of background picture or secular metaphysics, which gave an overall background meaning to life in general and to thinking about organisms in particular. It is significant, but surely telling, that for most of the period now being considered evolution was found less in academic departments in universities, and far more in museums and like institutions (Rainger, 1991). It was here that evolution made its home.

There are various reasons why evolution failed to rise right to the top. On the negative side, one must surely acknowledge that those people who were professionalizing biological science—this occurred around the time that the *Origin* was published, and the key figure was Thomas Henry Huxley—could see no real way in which evolution could be made into a self-supporting science (Desmond, 1994, 1997). Morphology, for instance, was being promoted as something which could be taught in the schools and which would therefore need a constant supply of teachers. Physiology was being promoted as something of essential value to physicians, and therefore likewise something which was justified from a pragmatic point of view. Evolution, however, simply did not seem to have this kind of potential for support: hence, for all that he portrayed himself as "Darwin's bulldog," evolution was rather downgraded by Huxley and by later professional biologists. More positively, people like Huxley were glad to make of evolution a popular science, as one might say, rather than a fully professional science. At this time, the third and fourth quarters of the nineteenth century, they were fighting what they saw to be the forces of reaction, particularly as represented by the Christian church (Desmond, 1997). Hence, they were happy to seize on what they saw as a perfect secular alternative, namely evolution with its story of origins, to challenge and match the Christian story of origins. Therefore, the professional biologists were only too happy to see evolution firmly located in such institutions as the American Museum of Natural History and the British Museum of Natural History: places where it could be used for socially edifying discourses and displays for the masses. Thanks to Darwin, therefore, evolution rose from the status of pseudoscience, but it did not rise above the status of popular science.

(I need to qualify this last statement a little. There was a Germanicized professional evolutionary morphology, obsessed with discerning phylogenies based on the fossil record and embryological analogies. But it was never a great success—there were far too many unknowns and anomalies—and all of the better and brighter young biologists went off into other fields, like cytology and genetics. This subject never became experimental, a failure connected—part cause and part effect—with the general failure of evolutionary thinking to rise above the level of popular science. Although everyone accepted evolution as fact, Darwin's mechanism of natural selection was not generally taken up, especially by practicing biologists. Morphologists and physiologists had little or no need of selection, so they did not run selection experiments. Relatedly, although no one actually denied natural selection, most supplemented or essentially replaced it with alternative mechanisms, including Lamarckism—the inheritance of acquired characters—and broader-based forces, like so-called orthogenetic momenta, pushing organisms ever higher and into more complex and baroque forms [Bowler, 1984, 1996].)

Things changed again around 1940, with the coming of the third and final phase of evolution's history. By about 1930, the newly discovered and developed theory of Mendelian genetics had been integrated mathematically with Darwinian selection, thanks to the population geneticists, R. A. Fisher (1930) and J.B.S. Haldane (1932) in England, and Sewall Wright (1931, 1932) in America. But much work then remained to be done, putting empirical flesh on the dry bones of the mathematical formalisms. This fell to a number of naturalistically oriented biologists, notably E.B. Ford (1964) and his school in England, and Theodosius Dobzhansky (1937) and his followers in America, particularly the ornithologist Ernst Mayr (1942), the paleontologist G.G. Simpson (1942), and the botanist G.L. Stebbins (1950). We find that there was a significant shift to a selection-based evolutionism, backed by thorough studies of populations in the wild as well as by experimental work done in the laboratory. But it was not just a question of improving the science as such. It was not just the epistemic factors which mattered. At the same time, the evolutionists of this age were much concerned to upgrade their science socially (Cain, 1992, 1994; Smocovitis, 1992, 1996). They formed societies, they founded journals, they moved back from the museums and into the universities. They sought out research grants, they found students, and they proselytized nonstop, particularly through a stunning series of beautifully crafted works.

This is not to say that the people who worked at this time—the people who founded what came to be known as the "synthetic theory of evolution" or "neo-Darwinism"—answered all the questions or solved all the problems. Indeed, the sixty years left in the century have shown that there was much work to be done. Many new areas were to be developed—for instance, the whole area of the evolution of social behavior remained to be opened and turned into what has become known as the sub-branch of "sociobiology" (Wilson, 1975). Many controversies were to be resolved—for instance, the whole question of the course of evolution at the macro level and whether one needs to supplement Darwinism with alternative ideas, like the paleontological theory of "punctuated equilibria," co-authored by Niles Eldredge and Stephen Jay Gould (1972). What one can say, however, is that finally, in this third period of evolutionary theory, one sees the ultimate realization of Charles Darwin's dream, that is to say, one sees a fully functioning, mature and professional area of science, moving forward in much the way that one finds forward movement in other areas of mature professional science, notably those in the physical and chemical sciences.

Obviously, there is much more that could be said about the history of evolutionary thought and there are many details waiting to be filled in. However, we have now enough before us from our case study to turn to the testing of our various hypotheses, and it is to this that we now proceed.

Testing the Hypotheses

The matter before us now is that of the putative relationship between evolutionary theorizing and the cultural or social value of progress. To start matters off, what can be said unequivocally is that there has long been a deep and intimate relationship between evolutionary theorizing and this cultural value. Indeed, it is not too much to say that evolutionary thought in the Enlightenment was the child of social views and hopes for progress (Ruse, 1996). People like Erasmus Darwin, in particular, believed very strongly that human beings could and were improving their lot through their own effort and intellectual powers. These progressionists then speculated that one would find an equivalent to social progress in the biological world, taking one from the most simple or primitive right up to the most complex or sophisticated (which was always identified with humankind). They then postulated not merely that one would find this kind of upward chain of being, to use an old term, but that it would be a dynamic chain, moving organisms up from the primitive to the complex, in what we would now call an evolutionary fashion. Usually having speculated that such progress could be found in the biological world, early evolutionists then turned around and used this as confirmation of their beliefs in social progress. The fact that this was as viciously circular as it was possible to be caused them no concerns whatsoever!

Progress was right there at the beginning. It was there in the work of Erasmus Darwin, it was also there in the work of Lamarck, who was deeply influenced by the French progressionists of the Enlightenment, the so-called philosophes (Richards, 1992). It was also one of the major reasons why Cuvier was so violently opposed to evolution (Outram, 1984). As a Christian, a Protestant no less, Cuvier was deeply committed to the idea of Providence, the belief that no overall change by human unaided hand or mind is possible. Everything ultimately rests in the hands of the Creator above. Again and again, therefore, we find Cuvier attacking evolution through what he saw as the soft underbelly of progress. And conversely, we find him going after progress by holding up to ridicule what he saw as the failed epistemic pretensions of evolutionism.

What relevance is any of this history to any of our hypotheses? No one, even the most hard-line objectivist, wants to deny that culture in general, and value-impregnated culture in particular, may be responsible for the formation of hypotheses. This indeed is the whole intent of the (already mentioned) hallowed distinction between the context of discovery and the context of justification. The context of discovery, as people like Popper have emphasized, can be as wild and culturally impregnated as you want. The point, argue these objectivists, is that as soon as scientists get serious and start thinking about reasonable grounds for their beliefs—as soon as scientists enter the context of justification—then the values slip away easily and quietly. The question we must now ask is not just whether or not progress was involved in the formation of evolutionism right at the beginning—indeed it was—but whether it persisted.

An easy question to answer! As you might imagine from the way I have described the history of evolutionism, speaking of it as being a pseudoscience right up to the time of Darwin, we find that progress persisted. If anything, towards the end of the first century of evolutionism's history it got even stronger. Take Chambers and his *Vestiges of the Natural History of Creation*. The very backbone of his theorizing is one of progress. As a very successful businessman, one who was much involved in the bringing of automated techniques to the printing trade, one might have expected Chambers to be an enthusiast for social and intellectual progress, and this he certainly was. More than this, he read his progress directly into his evolutionism and then—Erasmus Darwin fashion—used his evolutionism as a reason to justify his beliefs in social progress.

In short, this we can say categorically. For the whole of its first period of life, from the mid-eighteenth century to the time of the *Origin*, evolution was at the level of a pseudoscience. And progress was a fundamental part of the picture. Evolution was progressive. Evolution was used to justify progress. Moreover, as the reactions of critics like Cuvier show strongly, the status of evolution and its connection with progress were one and the same question. Evolution was seen to be a vehicle for a social ideology—which it was—and judged accordingly. Some liked it. Some did not. But all knew what it was. Hence, whatever the objectivist might expect or demand, there was simply no question of moving straight from a context of discovery to a context of justification: a move which would see the expulsion of the cultural or nonepistemic value of progress. Progress began as central and remained that way.

One might think therefore that at once we have a repudiation of H 1 (hypothesis one), that which sees cultural values going virtually immediately, and I suppose in a way we do. However, as you might imagine, the objectivist is going to be little troubled by the vanquishing of this hypothesis (at least my suspicion is the objectivist will claim to being little troubled by its supposed vanquishing). What will be argued is that nobody truly held to H 1 in its crude form. Rather everybody recognizes that cultural values are likely to persist in science, particularly at the beginning. However, the objectivist will argue, this is no reason then to give up the fight immediately and allow that the social constructivist is right. That is to say, to agree that H 2 is correct and that values stay unchanged and untroubled. Rather, the objectivist will argue that he or she was talking about "mature" or "professional" science, not something which I have openly labelled a "pseudoscience." Nobody wants to deny that pseudosciences are full of value ideas. Indeed, one of the major reasons that pseudosciences are pseudosciences is precisely because they are still stuck in the cultural and have not risen above it. Hence, they do not qualify as genuine science. So, H 1 is not refuted, because so far the theory of evolution does not apply to the hypothesis. Or if you prefer, one can say that H 1 in the crude form is now refuted, but that the objectivist truly held on to a variant of it. The objectivist (the sophisticated objectivist) held to H 3, that which allows that value connotations were there at the beginning, but which sees them being expelled gradually through the development of a science: a development as the science becomes more epistemic. That is to say, culture goes as the science starts to take more seriously things like predictive fertility and consilience. So at this point there is no reason to give way before H 2 (or H 4). Even if one rejects H 1, one can still go with H 3.

Back to history. What do we find with the coming of Darwin? We certainly find an upgrading of the epistemic (Ruse, 1979). Most particularly, as I have pointed out, we have the consilience right at the heart of Darwin's argument for the fact of evolution. And I should add we find that in other respects Darwin was sensitive to epistemic demands. For instance, consistency counted. Darwin was most concerned, when the physicists claimed that there was insufficient time for a mechanism like natural selection, to see how his biological theorizing could be reconciled with their claims. (In fact, Darwin was not very successful, but it turned out in this century that it was physics that was wrong, because it had omitted the vital factor of the warming effect of radioactive decay [Burchfield, 1974, 1975]. There is now quite enough time, from a viewpoint of physics, for such a mechanism as natural selection to operate.)

But do we find, as many supporters of H 3 would suggest, that the epistemic was used to expel the non-epistemic or cultural? Do we find that, because Darwin's theorizing now relied on natural selection, that thoughts of progress start to diminish? In fact, history suggests very much the opposite. If anything, after the Darwinian revolution progress rode higher than before! This was true even of those like Darwin who wanted to give natural selection a full and active role. This was even more true of the Spencer-inspired evolutionism that was popular right through to the end of the century. Although in the first edition of the *Origin* Darwin said relatively little about progress, by the third edition, he, like everyone else, was suggesting that evolution is progressive in the sense of leading up to humankind (Ospovat, 1981). Moreover, he offered an argument to the effect that natural selection brings about this progress: he argued that there will be what we today call "arms races" between competing lines, with the prey getting faster and the predator getting faster. Darwin thought that this kind of comparative progress will lead ultimately to a kind of absolute progress, namely, one which involves brains and intelligence and all sorts of human attributes.

In short, those who look to the history of evolutionary theory for a simple confirmation of H 3 are sadly mistaken in their expectations. The history just does not bear out at least the first part of the hypothesis about the relevance in natural selection. Having said this, however, I would not want to argue that H 3 is entirely irrelevant. As I have said, one does see an upgrading of evolutionary thought from the pseudo level, if not to the professional level at least to the popular level. This was undoubtedly in major part because of its increased epistemic virtues, things like consilience. At the same time, however, one sees that even evolutionists were happy to leave evolution at the less-than-highest levels, because it suited them to have a kind of secular metaphysics, or background, against which their theorizing could proceed. In other words, people were progressionists, but they were happy to see it in evolution, and to use evolution as a justification for their beliefs in social progress. There was therefore no simple and direct or automatic expulsion of the cultural by the epistemic as H 3 leads one to expect. At the same time, however, the hypothesis is surely correct in suggesting that the status of a theory is a function of its epistemic worth and of the extent to which it is culture-value impregnated. Evolutionary theory, for the second period of its history, did not achieve the highest levels and in major part this was because it was cultural-value impregnated. Progress was important and made much of by evolution, but there was a cost.

What about H 4? As evolution enters into its second phase, do we see in any sense the values—the cultural values—themselves starting to change? In fact, as is well known, towards the end of the nineteenth century many people started to think that social progress is by no means an assured phenomenon. They started to suspect that attempts to achieve social or cultural progress are liable to backfire in nasty and unforseen ways, for instance through such things as unemployment and pollution. In line with this point, to a certain extent we do find that H 4 is exemplified: by the end of the century, not a few evolutionists were starting to worry about degeneration and were pointing to cases of degeneration in the biological world to justify their social beliefs (Bowler, 1988; Lester, 1995). However, before one gets too excited, I must report that my findings are that in certain respects evolutionists, and perhaps scientists generally, constituted (perhaps still constitute) an atypical segment of society. It is by no means the case that evolutionists, in pointing to degeneration, were simply throwing up their hands and arguing that this is inevitable. Rather, they were pointing to degeneration as a dreadful warning as to what might happen to humankind unless we strive mightily to avoid it. In other words, my history-backed suspicion is that most, if not all, evolutionists were indeed (and continue to be) progressionists. It was just that they saw that progress is a lot less easy to achieve than they had hitherto suspected, and they used their biology to point this out.

We move on now to the coming of the third period of evolution's history, around 1940 when it is upgraded yet again: to the level of a mature or professional science. Here I would say we really do start to see the demise of H 2. One of the things that the synthetic theorists were particularly keen to do was to eliminate cultural values, and they saw progress as something they simply had to eliminate from their work. Interestingly, one who tried to have matters both ways was Julian Huxley, the grandson of Thomas Henry Huxley. In his major work, *Evolution: The Modern Synthesis* (1942), he tried to present a professional science, yet one which was progress-impregnated. Almost to a person, people turned against him and effectively excluded him from active participation in the community. People like Ford in England and Dobzhansky in America recognized that mature science has no place for cultural values: they therefore expelled progress from their science, or at least they tried to do so, and expected others to do likewise.

(Note that I am talking of the demise of H 2 in the context of my case study of progress. Many constructivists today would base their case for the applicability of H 2 to contemporary evolutionary theory on the basis of other factors—the theory's supposed sexism, for instance. I think that one can speak to these issues and that H 2 still fails for evolutionary theory, but these are matters for other places and other times. The strength and the weakness of the naturalistic approach is that one can deal with only one issue at a time.)

Before the objectivists start to celebrate that H 3 is now proven, apart from reminding them that the first part of their historical scenario (about selection expelling progress) is not well taken, let me also point out that the second part of their historical scenario (about Mendelian mutations expelling progress) is likewise not well taken. Although their successors were to wrestle with eliminating progress from their science, the mathematicians bringing Darwin together with Mendel had absolutely no problem with incorporating progress into their synthesis! In his seminal *The Genetical Theory of Natural Selection,* Fisher argued for what he called his "fundamental theorem of natural selection": he argued that there is an upward pressure, constantly forcing organisms up a progressive chain. Apparently, the nature of effective new mutations would be so small that selection could readily override any retrogressive effects that they would have. Consequently, far from the Darwin/Mendel synthesis in itself pointing away from progress, it was the essential underpinning foundation. Historically, it simply is not true that Darwinism expelled progress. It simply is not true that Mendelism did so either.

Nor, I might add, does history bear out the claim that the epistemic expelled the cultural: that the need to be predictive and consilient and the like expelled the hopes of progress. In fact, all of the synthetic theorists—Dobzhansky and Mayr and others (with the possible exception of E.B. Ford)—were themselves ardent progressionists. They all believed that evolution leads up, from the simple to the complex, ending ultimately in humankind (Dobzhansky, 1967; Stebbins, 1969; Simpson, 1949; Mayr, 1988). However, they all saw that incorporating a progressivist doctrine within their science would be antithetical to their hopes of achieving the status of professional scientists who would be sufficiently respected to be allowed into the universities, to be allowed graduate students, to gain grants, and so on. So they kicked progress out of their professional science. It was not the hope of being more epistemically successful that led to the diminution of the cultural within evolutionary biology. It was rather what one might call the values of the "internal culture" of science which led to the expulsion of the values of culture "external" to science: it was this which led to the cherishing of the epistemic. It was the desire to be taken seriously as professionals which led to the downgrading and expulsion of progress.

(Interestingly, the life and work of Cuvier suggests that this was not the first time that something like this had happened. As a modestly born Protestant in an increasingly conservative France, it was essential for Cuvier to portray science as culture free if he himself was to succeed within his culture. Only by showing that he was a practitioner of the one area of society where culture does not intrude could he then hope to be allowed to succeed and shine. I am not saying that Cuvier's work was, in fact, culture free: in fact I have suggested that with his commitment to Protestant Christianity, it almost certainly was not. But the point was it was essential for him to present it as being culture free. Something which he did very successfully.)

What I am suggesting, therefore, is that we would do best to formulate a fifth hypothesis.

H 5.

External cultural values go and epistemic values are promoted, but it is not a simple cause and effect relationship with epistemic values automatically pushing out cultural values. Rather, what we see are values internal to the culture of science becoming very important and expelling external cultural values, and promoting epistemic values. In terms of our case study, progress is expelled in the interests of achieving professional status.

The relationship between culture and the epistemic, therefore, is far more complex than one might have believed before the case study was examined in detail: values internal to the culture of science are used to expel cultural values of society (values external to science) and to promote epistemic values. What then of H 2 and H 4? If indeed (external) cultural values are expelled, not because they are now rejected but because it is expedient that they be promoted for the cause of other desired ends, might we not expect to find that sometimes this culture will continue to intrude into science, particularly if the practitioners still believe in it? Or might we not, in addition, expect to find, as H 4 suggests, that particularly in this age when progress is so derided by intellectuals, that values will persist but these values will be anti-progressionist?

My suspicion would be that perhaps some cultural values could and do persist, despite practitioners' avowed intent. I do not mean to exaggerate. One might well expect that new generations of evolutionists would have internalized the non-progressivist nature of their subject and so feel little need to bring progress in. But this may not be a general rule. In fact, I suggest that is what one finds. The younger breed of evolutionist has little interest in bringing external cultural values into science and indeed a measure of contempt for those that do. This is not a reflection of the change of external values but of the internalization of the cultural values of science itself. There is no place for society in a professional discipline. Older evolutionists—the generation who may still have come to evolution because of their progressionism—are torn. Here, one might and does find progressivist sentiments persisting: sometimes, indeed, proudly portrayed. For instance, John Maynard Smith, the doyen of evolutionists in Britain, is an avowed progressionist and still writes in this vein (Maynard Smith and Szathmary, 1995). Likewise, Edward O. Wilson (1992, 1994), the leading Darwinian evolutionist and sociobiologist in America, is an ardent progressionist and not beyond putting forth his positive views on this subject. (Although interestingly, Wilson recognizes that frank rows of progress in professional work will gain him little credit and tends now to put forward his progressionism in his more popular writings.)

Interestingly, I find that the atypical nature of scientists within society persists. Although it may indeed be the case that most intellectuals are not progressionists, and although it is the case that the younger practitioners no longer think it appropriate to bring it into their science, scientists continue to be fairly positive about progress (Wagar, 1972). I suspect that there are reasons for this, most particularly that science is the one area of human inquiry where one gets real change (or, if you prefer, the appearance of real change). Scientists really do make discoveries and this emboldens them to think that they are making progress: a view which they then generalize to culture as a whole, and subsequently read into evolution. In other words, although in evolutionary writings one does get some sepulchral warnings about degeneration, generally speaking, evolutionists are positive towards progress and as (one might expect) one does find that—even in the writings of those who want to keep it out—this sometimes seeps through. However, in general line with my new and final hypothesis, H 5, my suspicion and finding is that contemporary evolutionary theory promotes the epistemic and tries hard to eliminate or downplay the cultural: that is to say the culture external to science. (Peter Medawar is a nice confirmation. He was an enthusiast for scientific progress—for cultural progress generally—yet he was absolutely scathing about Julian Huxley's [1959] endorsement of Teilhard de Chardin's progressive evolutionism. See Medawar [1961] and then Medawar [1972].)

Conclusion

So what does my naturalistic study tell us about the objectivity/subjectivity of science? It certainly shows that things are a lot more interesting and complex than one might have thought just by *a priori* speculation! So, if only for this reason, it surely is self-justifying. But does it lead us to any firm conclusions?

My own feeling is that the study certainly gives no comfort to the extreme subjectivist, the ardent social constructivist. In the history of evolutionary theory, we see a clear and definitive move towards objectivity: where this is to be understood in terms of the use and exemplification in the epistemic virtues of such things as predictive accuracy, fertility, consistency, consilience, and so forth. At the same time, we see a definite desire to eliminate the cultural, and an ongoing process of putting this desire into effect. To pretend that the work of today's evolutionists is of the same epistemic/cultural standing as the work of Erasmus Darwin or Jean Baptiste de Lamarck is mainly to show that social construction holds of philosophy if not of science. There is no question but things have changed dramatically.

However, were one simply to end here with the objectivist triumphant, one would be guilty of grave distortion. Apart from the occasional persistence—overtly or covertly—of the cultural of society, there is little doubt but that in another sense non-epistemic values do continue to shape the nature of evolutionary biology. I refer now to the values internal to the culture of science, like the desire to be treated as a professional in the physical sciences, with all that that entails. To be candid, I am not quite sure what this all means or implies. My hunch is that one should start to look with some suspicion on claims that the epistemic values are, as it were, logically, or in some other conceptual way, necessary conditions for thinking about the world. That they are *a priori* or Platonic forms of some kind, written in stone and existing eternally, independent of human thought processes. Given that they have almost a status of expediency rather than outside logical compulsion, my suspicion is that the values have a much more human face than many philosophers think: that they may themselves be embedded in human nature in some wise.

Whether this embedding be purely cultural, or genetic, as the sociobiologists would suggest, or some combination, or indeed something else, is another matter. I am not saying that the epistemic values are purely arbitrary—they certainly work pragmatically at some level. But I am suggesting that their adoption seems to have human-driven desires and values. Which leads me to suspect that although one might properly speak of science as being objective, in the sense of above and beyond the vagaries of culture on a day-to-day basis, at some deeper and more profound level, science is itself a thoroughly human product. In other words, although the subjectivists or social constructivists are wrong in their detailed arguments, they have nevertheless grasped a profound insight about the nature of science. Just as science is truly objective, so also is it truly subjective (Ruse, 1999)!

These are all suspicions rather than proven points, so let me conclude by coming back to Don Campbell. I think he would applaud the kind of naturalistic enterprise in which I have been engaged. I suspect he would have searching questions about its execution. I know that he would think my conclusion profoundly unsatisfying and incomplete. He would surely be pushing me hard on whether I think epistemic values are truly cultural or truly genetic or how they might be some combination of the two. He would be less interested in what I have done than in what I ought to do. He would be urging me not to rest, but to get on with the job which lies before me. We would end by agreeing that I am not yet finished, with my admission that I am aware of the work that lies ahead. I cannot now promise him in person that I will keep at this inquiry as long as I am able. All I can do is make my pledge to his memory. Not much, but the best tribute one can offer to one such as Donald Campbell.

6

Nested Hierarchies of Vicarious Selectors

Kyung-Man Kim

Introduction

"Am I acting too bossy?" was the remark that Donald Campbell made after a long discussion about my Ph. D. dissertation which is now published as a book (Kim, 1994a). In contrast to what he said, Don was so kind and open-minded that I could tell him everything that I had in mind, even though it was the first time that I met him. And during our discussion, Don made coffee for us, which was, however, too strong for me to drink. So I asked him, "Why do you drink such strong coffee?" He gave me an unexpected answer. "I am so old that I can't stay alert without drinking the strongest coffee I can make. How can I read all the books and articles that I wake up to find every morning without staying alert?"

It was probably due to such intellectual passion and open-mindedness that, unlike his contemporaries Robert Merton and Edward Shils, who disregarded the newly emerging sociology of science led by the young relativists, Campbell was more than willing to read their works carefully, and engaged in a series of critical dialogue with the relativist sociologists of science. As can be seen from the title of his last paper, "From Evolutionary Epistemology via Selection Theory to Sociology of Scientific Validity" (Campbell, 1997), for the last fifteen years before his death, Campbell was concerned with developing what he called a "sociology of scientific validity" in which he attempted a "dialectical synthesis" of his selection theory with the social constructivist view of science.

As I shall show below, in contrast to the social constructivist approach, such a synthesis explicitly raises the question of "validity" in science and provides an answer as to how the social system of science can improve its collective belief in the validity-enhancing direction. I hope that, being a logical extension of Campbell's attempt to work out what he calls a "sociology of scientific validity," this paper can contribute to the completion of Campbell's unfinished project.

For his last thirty years Campbell was concerned with developing the "blind-variation-and-selective-retention" paradigm (BVSR) for the explanation of the fit between a system and its environment, and its application to the wide range of phenomena, from sociocultural evolution to scientific change (Campbell, 1965a, 1974b, 1977). Heavily influenced by the development of modern cybernetics, Campbell takes seriously the BVSR process as the universal "non-teleological" explanation of the teleological achievement, or a fit of a system to its environment, since, otherwise, we have to accept the Leibnizian pre-established harmony. Thus, for Campbell, even the Darwinian principle of variation and natural selection for the explanation of the organic evolution is but one example of this universal paradigm. Campbell argues that before any system-environment fit occurs three requirements have to be met: (1) blind variation, (2) selection among variations, and (3) preservation or propagation of variations.

Critics of Campbell, however, argue that scientific evolution cannot be subsumed under this universal paradigm (Ruse, 1983, 1986; Skagestad, 1978). For these critics, problem solving in science is anything but "blind" or "random." Indeed, even some of the advocates of the evolutionary perspective on scientific development subscribe to the view that conceptual variations in science are biased to or "coupled" (Toulmin, 1972) with the correct solution of the problems under investigation. In emphasizing the "teleological" character of scientific achievement, however, they fail to come up with a mechanistic explanation of the marvelous adaptations of conceptual variations to scientific problems. In this chapter, I will do three things. First, by clarifying and making ample use of the important concept of the "nested hierarchy of vicarious selection process" (Campbell, 1959, 1960; see also Kim, 1997), I will show that the criticism leveled against the BVSR analogy of scientific change is essentially wrongheaded. Second, I will argue that scientific evolution, like biological evolution, is subject to the BVSR process. Third, by using a concrete example, I will show that the BVSR model of scientific evolution necessarily leads us to adopt what I call the "symmetrical-social selection" theory of scientific validity.

Blind Variation and Selective Retention as Knowledge Process

> I regard this idea of the "blindness" of trials in a trial-and-error movement as an important step beyond the mistaken idea of random trials.
>
> —Karl Popper

For Campbell, knowing is always profoundly indirect and presumptive. In order to indicate such a "presumptive" nature of knowledge acquisition, Campbell used the term "vicarious selectors." By using two of Campbell's favorite examples, let me briefly discuss the concept of vicarious selectors. First, while our eyes seem to give us "direct" and reliable knowledge in the normal environment, they sometimes delude us in abnormal environments. Consider fog and glass as two such abnormal environments. While glass is transparent, it is nevertheless impenetrable; and while fog is opaque, it is nevertheless penetrable. The "presumption" that anything transparent is penetrable (and vice versa) is violated in such abnormal environments. Evolved in an environment in which glass and fog have been rare, our vision—a vicarious selector which substitutes for the direct collision with the external objects—deludes us in an ecology which is not typical of the history of the human evolution (Campbell, 1974b).

The second example more vividly illustrates the nature of vicarious selection process. The leg of a lizard, when amputated, regrows to a length optimal for locomotion and survival. Such an optimal adjustment process however never implies the "direct" fit of the organism with its environment. Rather it shows that the leg length is controlled by the "internalized" or "vicarious" selector which is built into the developmental system of the lizard. But, being the product of previous natural selection, such a vicarious selector has "historicity" (Campbell, 1997) and only works with the *presumption* that the ecology under which it is developed remains the same. Under changing environment, therefore, the vicarious selector might not work any more and will be subject to the more encompassing natural selection.

Both our vision and the reference signal built into the developmental system of the lizard have been "originally" obtained through such an "inductive process" which Campbell dubbed the "blind-variation-and-selective-retention" process. Thus, in the lizard example, reference signal which has been kept tuned to the previous ecological conditions is subject to the BVSR process in a changing environment.

> The larger, encompassing selection system is the ecological organism-environment interaction. Nested in a hierarchical way within it is the selective system directly operating on leg length, the "setting" or criteria for which are themselves subject to natural selection. What are criteria at one level are but "trial" of the criteria of the next higher, more fundamental, more encompassing, less frequently invoked level. (Campbell, 1970, p. 55)

Campbell further argues that we can build the nested hierarchy of knowledge process in terms of the vicarious selectors which are ordered according to the amount of the *vicariousness* or *presumptiveness* incorporated into the selectors. Starting from the genetic adaptation as the lowest (i.e., most fundamental) level in the hierarchy, with increasing order, he enumerates various levels of vicarious selectors including nonmnemonic problem solving (direct locomotion without memory), vicarious locomotor devices, habit-instinct, visually guided thought, mnemonically guided or supported thought, social learning, language, and finally science, which is but one aspect of sociocultural evolution. For example, consider the nested hierarchy between "nonmnemonic problem solving" and "vicarious locomotor device" such as distance receptor of an organism. At the level of nonmnemonic problem solving, an organism (e.g., bacteria) would engage in a random change of locomotor direction until a setting that is nourishing is found. Here the cessation of the locomotor activity is the "retention" phase of the three step formula. At this point, the random locomotor activity (i.e., trial and error) of the organism through full movements and collision comes to an end without retaining what is learned in memory.

Substituting for spatial exploration by random trial and error are various distance receptors. These can be regarded as vicarious locomotor devices, substituting for more fundamental locomotor collision with solid external objects. The constraint or presumptive assumption present at this level of vicarious knowledge process is that the reflective opaqueness of the wave band emitted by the organism *vicariously* represents the locomotor impenetrability of the objects. Namely, the organism assumes that those objects with reflective opaqueness to the wave which he emits are "in fact" impenetrable (Campbell, 1974b, p. 424). This assumption can be reconfirmed only by its overt locomotion and collision. Thus the increase of vicariousness in going up the hierarchical ladder means that the higher-level vicarious selectors presuppose, although presumptively, the validity of the already evolved wisdom at the higher, more fundamental level. This, in turn, means that, beyond the range of the problems for which the constrained processes are adequate, one has no choice but to "blindly" explore the unknown portion of the world.

In this connection, largely agreeing with the biological interpretation of Kantian *a priori* forms of intuition and categories of experience as the products of phylogenetic adaptation (Lorenz, 1962), Popper (1972) similarly argues that we are born with dispositions or knowledge which can be expressed in the form of expectations about the external world. Plugged into Campbell's vicarious selection theory, Popper's contention means that, given the necessary imperfection of our internal representation of the external world which is the product of the previous natural selection, we have no choice but to theorize or hypothesize vicariously the still unknown external world. Put in other words, this means that, on the basis of the already achieved wisdom of the external environment, we make conjectures about the unknown portions of the external environment. Thus Popper argues quite correctly that we have innate dispositions or inborn inclination to hypothesize in a certain way (i.e., we have inborn expectation about the world) only to be corrected by our experience.

Under the umbrella term "Darwinian epistemology," Michael Ruse (1986) elaborates and defends the view that the nature and development of science are constrained and based on the biologically evolved cognitive power of human beings which is obtained through human beings' ongoing struggle for survival and reproduction. Borrowing the term "epigenetic rules" from Lumsden and Wilson (1981) to indicate what he regards as the evolutionarily acquired cognitive power of human beings, Ruse, I think, successfully shows that even the most abstract scientific theories are, in the ultimate sense, built on the epigenetic rules. Rather than repeat his argument here, I will consider what I find the most interesting aspect of his discussion. Though he does not make explicit reference to the "hierarchy of vicarious selectors," when he discusses the adoption of the non-Euclidean geometry in Einstein's theory of relativity in response to the false predictions produced by the traditional system based on the traditional mathematics and logic he explicitly invokes the hierarchical nature of vicarious selectors. Namely, rather than preserving Euclidean geometry which yields false predictions, scientists adopted non-Euclidean geometry in order to preserve the logical principle known as Modus tollens, a kind of epigenetic rule which, according to Ruse, is acquired through human beings' struggle for survival. Thus:

> [I]t shows that we recognize an *ordering* among them. We would rather stick with modus tollens than with Euclidean geometry, if the choice be forced upon us. . . . [Y]ou expect some rules to be more powerful than others. (Ruse, 1986, p. 171, italics added)

What Ruse is arguing here is that when the two vicarious selectors of different levels are in conflict we would hold on to the more general, fundamental, and evolutionarily earlier vicarious selector (which are closer to environment and hence more fundamental). Here the outputs of the less fundamental level are fed back into the more general, and fundamental vicarious selectors in order to arrive at an appropriate decision. Like an amputated lizard in a new environment for which the previous reference signal (or vicarious selector) for optimal leg length no longer provides adequate information as to the optimal leg length, given the principle known as Modus tollens, Einstein has to blindly search for the solution which can substitute for the traditional solution. Having clarified the hierarchical nature of the vicarious selection process, I now want to consider the criticisms leveled against the blind variation thesis and see if these criticisms can stand up to scrutiny.

Blind Variations at the Level of Individual Scientists

The foregoing discussion leads us to expect that, as a problem solver, men are not different from lower organisms. The evolutionarily acquired and phylogenetically transmitted capacity for cognition and learning are the same for all human beings. Hence, as Vollmer's (1984) concept of mesocosm indicates, we are particularly well adapted to the perception of medium-sized objects. More recently, the study of the cognitive limitation of human beings has been termed as the evolutionary epistemology of cognitive mechanism (Bradie, 1986).

However, when considering an individual scientist as a problem solver, in addition to those factors that are found in human beings' common evolutionary background we find numerous factors which act as vicarious selectors and therefore impinge on the generation and selection of his or her conceptual variations. While working with the generally accepted theories and data available in a specific period, each individual scientist nevertheless learns from his or her own research and data and develops his or her own conception of good selection criteria (i.e., his or her own vicarious selectors which are at best fallibly and presumptively obtained) which aid him or her in selecting from among many conceptual variations of his or her own. These "peculiar" vicarious selectors of an individual scientist which act and select as vicarious thought environment (i.e., environment as selectors against which thought trials are tested) are in turn shaped by his or her peculiar intellectual background, training, research experience, local culture of a specific laboratory, and perhaps by his or her social philosophy and interests (Barnes, 1982; Bloor, 1976; Shapin, 1979).

When pressed for a solution of a particular intellectual problem, a scientist generates a number of thought as well as experimental trials to find a solution of that problem. In doing so, he or she can narrow down the search space by using previous research findings which are based on the models, theories, and inscription devices (Latour and Woolgar, 1979) available at that time. However, beyond such *constrained* processes, he or she has to blindly search for the solution of the new problem. What does "blindly" exactly mean here? Collins's (1985) study of laser building vividly shows why we should regard the experimental trials and adjustments involved in the building of a "working" laser as essentially blind. When Bob Harrison, who succeeded in building his first laser called a TEA laser, later tried to build another kind of laser, he found that his knowledge about his first laser was not enough to build a different one. As the laser continued to refuse to work, a shadow of uncertainty crept in and Harrison had to test all sorts of things—changing the gas mixture and the electrode separation, etc.—that he had taken for granted up to that time. This means that the tacit knowledge that he developed through his first laser building experience—i.e., in our terminology, vicarious selection criteria—did not work any more. What is interesting about Collins's study is that only *after* he succeeded in building a "working" laser, could Harrison establish the "correct way of seeing" the problem (Collins, 1985, p. 76). Before the laser worked, therefore, Harrison could not judge whether the various trials and adjustments were nothing worth bothering about, or significant. *In short, before the laser worked, any of his trials were no more likely to be correct than the others.*

Having clarified the notion of "blindness," let me now examine whether the criticisms leveled against the BVSR thesis can withstand scrutiny. Ruse's survey over this field concludes with the following remark:

> [B]ut my . . . opinion was that the disanalogies are so great that probably any attempt to view scientific theory change through the lens of the Darwinian evolutionism does more harm than good. I have myself seen no reason to change that opinion. (1983, p. 151)

Since, as I will show, the selection theory advocated in this paper is exclusively based on the BVSR algorithm and not on a complex analogy with biological evolution (e.g., Toulmin, 1972; Shrader, 1980; Richards, 1981), I will concern myself only with Ruse's attack on the BVSR thesis. To begin with, consider the following argument of Ruse:

> The building blocks of organic evolution are random. At least, the building blocks of science, the new variants, are anything but random. At least . . . it is certainly the case that most new ideas come only as a result of major directed effort, and they are in turn directed, or *designed* for the task at hand. (1983, p. 143, italics added)

This quote shows that Ruse fails to understand the implication of the vicarious selection process. As I have indicated above, the conceptual space of Bob Harrison in which his thought and experimental trials are made and against which these trials were evaluated was constrained by his previous knowledge about his first laser. And, insofar as he uses this knowledge base to build the second one, his trials cannot be said to be completely random. Also, I do not deny that Harrison made a "directed" effort to solve his problems. But, as Collins persuasively demonstrated, beyond the range of problems for which his previous knowledge is appropriate, Harrison's previous knowledge did not help him at all to remove his troubles. Only after he solved his problem could Harrison find an explanation as to why he was so stupid! As has been pointed out by many evolutionary theorists, the originality of Darwin's concept of natural selection lies in its "non-teleological" (or causal) explanation of the teleological achievement (Wimsatt, 1972; see also Giere, this volume). But since Ruse emphasizes only the teleological character of scientific achievement and fails to come up with a better scenario than the BVSR process, he himself must be accused of being unscientific.

Teleology, Symmetry, and the Social Selection Theory of Scientific Validity

As we have seen above, at least in his 1983 paper, Ruse apparently did not recognize the importance of blind fumbling on the part of individual scientists, and wrongly emphasized the "designed" nature of the fit between scientific theories and the intellectual problems, and the radical disanalogy between organic and scientific variations. However, in his book (Ruse 1986), he apparently *admits* that individual scientists fumble blindly until they produce scientific variations which will eventually enter the "public" pool of science. However, Ruse does not give up his conviction on the disanalogy and thinks that he puts his finger on the lethal defect inherent in Campbell's move to patch up the science/organism analogy:

> [E]ven if Campbell's position were entirely correct . . . he would locate the supposedly Darwinian element in science at the wrong point to save the organism/science analogy, as it is usually conceived. Campbell argues that the Darwinian process in science *occurs in the production of variations*, before they get into the public pool of science. By the time Watson and Crick published their model, expectedly it had a *direct look* about it, because by then the "blind-variation-and-selective-retention" was finished. But in the world of organisms, it is these just-appearing-in-public-variations which are random. (Ruse, 1986, p. 59, italics added)

In penning this paragraph, Ruse again displayed his serious misunderstanding about the BVSR process in science. Ruse's allegedly new critique of the science/organism analogy is here directed to show the existence of the "preselection mechanism" (or what I have called individual vicarious selection) in science which sifts the useless variations but which cannot be found in organic evolution. However, Ruse's preoccupation with the refutation of the analogy between organic and scientific variations misleads him to neglect the "existing constraints" (genetic, anatomical, etc.) which affect the range of possible variations that are possible. Therefore he argues as if biological variation were completely random in the sense that anything can emerge from the existing characteristics of the species. Just as the generation as well as the selection of the thought trials are constrained by the vicarious explorations in a vicarious thought environment, so the genetic background and the peculiarities of the species in question constrain, and in that sense preselect, the range of possible variations.

However, Ruse thinks that such a rebuttal is merely another attempt to patch up the already helpless science/organism analogy, for it leaves the core of his criticism intact, that is, despite the existence of the preselection mechanism in science, how can Campbell argue that in-public variations in science are blind? More laconically, this objection comes down to this: all the confusion is due to Campbell's (and my) failure to distinguish between something "being unknown" and something "being haphazard" (1986, pp. 59–60). According to Ruse, nobody can be prescient and hence nobody knows what the correct solution of the problem will turn out to be. But Ruse hastens to add that this does *not* logically entail that our search process and its results are haphazard. For the search process takes place within a constrained space, and hence, even when the search results turn out to be incorrect, it cannot be said that those results are haphazard. Since I have discussed at length why conceptual variations at the individual level are not haphazard or random but blind, the problem now comes down to whether the term "blind" can be consistently applied to the selection of variations even *after* the preselected variations entered the public pool of science.

To answer this question, let me now turn to Ruse's argument that the Darwinian process in science—that is, the BVSR process—is finished *before* Watson and Crick's solution enter the public pool of science. This means that once the BVSR process of Watson and Crick came to an end, it ended once and for all. But, as I will show below, in contrast to Ruse's argument, the Darwinian process—or BVSR process—occurs not just before the variations get into the public pool of science but also *after* they entered the public pool of science.

To show why this is so, let me now shift our analytical focus from individual scientists such as Watson and Crick to the community of scientists. In discussing Watson and Crick's discovery, Ruse argues as if there were no DNA models that competed with Watson and Crick's. That is, paying his attention only to the theory which *turns out to be correct*, Ruse disregards many conceptual variations which eventually turned out to be incorrect and argues as if Watson and Crick's model did not have to undergo another selection process at the level of scientific community. This is precisely why Ruse argues that once the BVSR process of Watson and Crick comes to an end, their model has a "direct" look about the structure of DNA. Insofar as we accept Ruse's argument, we also have to accept that the term "direct" logically implies that Watson and Crick were *clairvoyant* as to the fate of their theory. But how did Watson and Crick know *in advance* that their model would be accepted by the community of scientists? Clearly,

Ruse is here making use of a judgment that is available only with "hindsight," that is, only after the selection process at the community level is finished. If he is to avoid using hindsight and teleology, therefore, Ruse has to admit that the Darwinian process also occurs *after* the preselected variations entered the public pool of science.

The above discussion shows that BVSR process occurs once again after the preselected variations of individual scientists enter the public pool of science. Before the selection process at the community level is completed, any of the competing models including Watson and Crick's, however direct and clairvoyant these models appear to their inventors, *are no more likely to be correct than the others.* Thus the essential connotation of the term blind is that the variations preselected by the individual scientists are independent of the selection environment.[1]

What emerges from the above discussion is that we should reject the "teleological model" of conceptual adaptation in which attention is paid only to the development of the successful theory at the individual level. Since in this model the truth of the now accepted theory is taken for granted or regarded as self-evident, it is not necessary to explain why the theory has been accepted by the scientific community. As a consequence, in Ruse's account of the discovery of DNA, we are not told why and how Watson and Crick's theory came to be selected from the pool of competing theories. In contrast to the teleological model of Ruse, in the so-called symmetrical model (Bloor, 1976), we avoid using hindsight and treat both currently accepted and rejected theories *impartially*, i.e., as "unjustified" blind variations, and a particular effort is made to show how and why a specific theory comes to be selected (and hence validated) from the pool of competing theories.

While the practitioners of the sociology of scientific knowledge (SSK) rightly insist that we should bracket our judgment as to the truth and falsity of the contending knowledge claims, and treat them merely as "unjustified" theories, they nevertheless fail to show why and how one of those unjustified theories came to be accepted by the majority of scientists through their argumentative process. As I have shown elsewhere, in most of their sociological studies of scientific controversies, they did not show "how an asymmetry (i.e., consensus change) emerges out of the 'symmetrical opposition' of the contending parties with the lapse of time" (Kim, 1994b, p. 399, 1994a).

What then would a "symmetrical-social selection theory" of scientific change look like? Let me illustrate how the model actually works by using a critical dialogue between a historian of science and a sociologist of scientific knowledge. In his review of Martin Rudwick's book *The Great Devonian Controversy* (1985), Trevor Pinch (1986) argues that Rudwick's narrative account of the closure of the controversy violates the principle of symmetry by taking only one side of participants' account and ignores the arguments of the two "marginal" geologists, Thomas Weaver and David Williams, who never assented to the emerging consensus on the Devonian interpretation. According to Pinch, rather than establish the "marginality" of Weaver and Williams through the detailed analysis of the dynamic evolution of the controversy, Rudwick "use[s] the marginal status of these scientists [Weaver and Williams] . . . as the basis for not taking their arguments seriously." Pinch thus argues that Rudwick has never been attentive to Weaver's and Williams's own arguments which, for Weaver and Williams at least, "were perfectly respectable" (Pinch, 1986, p. 712). In short, Pinch complains that Rudwick assumes the "marginal" status of Weaver and Williams from the beginning of his analysis and uses the marginal status of these two geologists to justify his neglect of their arguments.

If Pinch is right, Rudwick should be accused of providing an asymmetric and teleological account of the closure of the Devonian controversy. The question, therefore, comes down to whether Rudwick, in fact, fails to show how and why Weaver's and Williams's view came to be marginalized by the majority of the participants of the controversy with the lapse of time. But in reconstructing the emergence of consensus in the research network of the nineteenth century geologists, Rudwick has been particularly attentive to the symmetrical treatment of the contrasting views, and endeavors to show how and why a consensual view eventually emerged through the negotiations of the meaning of empirical evidence by the participants of the controversy. In contrast to Pinch's argument, Rudwick demonstrates that Weaver's and Williams's view were taken seriously by their opponents (e.g., Murchison, Sedgwick, and others) at some point during the controversy (Rudwick, 1985, pp. 78–80, 332–342). Rudwick further demonstrates that, regardless of Weaver's and Williams's subjective convictions on the validity of their own views, their views came to be judged to be patently implausible as the controversy evolved, and finally, when the consensus emerged, no one took their arguments seriously. From the community's viewpoint, their solutions were, to use our terminology, merely two of those "blind" variations that had to be winnowed for the emergence of a new consensus. Hence, in contrast to Pinch's argument that Rudwick dismisses Weaver's and Williams's views by relegating them to the marginalized position without an explanation, Rudwick shows that the marginalization of Weaver's and Williams's views was the *consequence* rather than the *cause* of the closure of the controversy.

The foregoing discussion shows that the "symmetrical social selection" theory is not concerned with individual epistemic competence but with the specification of the social mechanism of "winnowing" rival conceptual variations at the collective level. While acknowledging SSK practitioners' emphasis on the local laboratory culture and practice, social interests, the power structure and the clique formation in the scientific community as important social selectors of scientific theory, the symmetrical social selection model proposes to examine how—to borrow Pierre Bourdieu's term—such social struggles for power, capital, and dominance are "converted" into the advancement of knowledge through the crisscrossing critique of each other's intellectual product (Bourdieu, 1991; see also Hull, 1978). Following the tradition in which Popper, Merton, and Campbell participate, the symmetrical social selection theory, therefore, passes the justificatory buck not to the individual scientists' efforts to be objective and impartial, i.e., to the individual vicarious selection process but to the selection environment that consists of various social, cognitive, and historical factors.[2]

There are at least two sociological-historical studies of scientific change which adopt the perspective I have called a symmetrical social selection theory of scientific validity (Rudwick, 1985; Kim, 1994a). In these studies particular stress is placed on the social process in which the organized distribution of authority and control within the scientific community, the shifting allegiance of the participants through clique formations, and conformity pressures press participants' inference one way rather than another, and hence affect the evolving outcome of the controversies. Along with such social selectors of belief, these studies also seek to show how the physical world as reflected in the research data serves an "editing function" by contributing to the process of selection of more valid and more real theory. By delineating the social process in which scientists with different theoretical orientations stay together in a focused disputation, attending and monitoring each other's arguments and advancing the "best" evidence and arguments, and thereby keeping each other honest, these two studies show how a theory with improved validity is selected from the rival conceptual variations put forward to explain the natural phenomena in question.

Conclusion

The symmetrical social selection theory of scientific validity places heavy emphasis on the selection of variation at the collective level. For, from the viewpoint of the scientific community, individual variations are still "unjustified" variations. And the problem of understanding collective appraisal of scientific innovations (or variations) necessarily requires the sociological theory of idea winnowing. Underlying the symmetrical social selection theory is the idea that, like the successful theories, the rejected theories were also worked out by intelligent, purposeful scientists. Thus, until the selection process at the community level is finished, successful and rejected theories are both equally blind trials. From the scientific community's viewpoint, what Ruse calls "in-public variations" are blind. Ruse's revised critique of the BVSR paradigm for scientific change failed to capture this important point. This paper explores the way in which a theory with improved validity is selected from such blind variations by adopting a sociological perspective.

Notes

I was fortunate to have Donald Campbell's valuable comments on an earlier version of this article. I am also grateful to David Hull for his comments on an earlier draft of this chapter.

1. David Hull mounted essentially the same criticism. He put his query this way.

> *Ruse:* Scientists do not search for solutions to problems blindly because they develop their hypotheses on the basis of all sorts of knowledge and in anticipation of certain possible solutions. Of course, they do not know in advance what the correct solution will turn out to be. They are not clairvoyant.

> *Kim:* Scientists search for solutions to problems blindly even though they develop their hypotheses on the basis of all sorts of knowledge and in anticipation of certain possible solutions because they do not know in advance what the correct solution will turn out to be. They are not clairvoyant.

Like Ruse, Hull thinks that all the confusion is due to my failure to effectively distinguish between something "being unknown" and something "being haphazard." However, in paraphrasing Ruse's position, Hull did not recognize that Ruse, in fact, argues that scientists are "clairvoyant." For, as I have argued above, focusing exclusively on the theory which later turns out to be successful, Ruse argues that, once it is shown how this theory is selected by an individual scientist, it is not necessary to show why this theory is selected by the wider community of scientists. That is why Ruse argues that, once their blind fumbling came to an end, Watson and Crick's theory had a "direct look" about the structure of DNA. In such an account, however, it is required that Watson and Crick have the *foresight* that their solution will be selected by the scientific community. And this shows that their theory is *not* independent of the conditions of the selection environment.

2. Giere (this volume) also writes that Campbell's insistence that descriptive epistemology be psychological, sociological, and evolutionary is in line with his naturalistic epistemology that proposes to analyze the social and cognitive mechanisms responsible for the growth and decline of a research program.

7

Social Constructions and Evolution

Henry Plotkin

I was privileged on one occasion to be chided, albeit gently, by Don Campbell for flirting with what he called non-entitivitiness in the form of Bohm's concepts of process and stages of order (Plotkin, 1987). Guilty as I was, this essay is written as an act of contrition to the memory of a great man. I seek redemption by considering how something so seemingly immaterial as social facts, or what I prefer to call social constructions, can be placed within the province of natural science. I follow Searle (1995) in defining social constructions as social facts "where the facts exceed the physical features of the underlying physical reality" (p. 228). The archetypal example is money. A $50 note has a value far exceeding that of the paper and dyes making up the note. Its value lies in agreement between people as to just what it is worth—a theatre ticket, a couple of books, or whatever. This is "collective intentionality," to use Searle's nice phrase.

Campbell was an eminent social psychologist and also one of the founding fathers of modern evolutionary epistemology, though he came to dislike the latter phrase (Campbell, 1997). Being both of these was to be subject to a rich and potent mix of ideas, to which the fertile breadth of his writings bears witness. The result was that one of the constant themes running through Campbell's work is how to marry the social and biological sciences, which, of course, is one of the great challenges left to contemporary science. Thus Campbell would, I think, have been both interested and amused at the outrageous juxtapositioning of the terms in the title of this essay. Nothing could be of greater significance for the synthesis he sought than the biologizing of social constructions. What follows is the merest sketch, which should be read as a series of questions, since we do not yet have any answers; it is just the beginnings of a project which attempts to show the way towards a natural science account of the evolution of the human capacity for entering into social constructions. The brevity of the piece as well as the limitations of the author are guarantee of a lack of exhaustive treatment of the subject. I shall lay emphasis on just one set of questions, and place some markers on other possible routes to understanding.

Some History

Social scientists are still wont to use culture as a talisman against what they see as the depredations of a powerful and reductivist biology, even though it is approaching half a century since Kroeber (1953), one of the inheritors from Boas of the cultural anthropologists' crown, accepted that culture is "wholly part of nature," and that it is "going to be somebody's business to deal scientifically" with culture. One of the beginnings of the incorporation of the study of human culture into the natural sciences, which is what I take Kroeber's "scientifically" to mean, was Murdock's (1956) suggesting the possibility of applying selection theory to account for the transformation of cultures in time, which Campbell (e.g., 1965a) was later to build on. These were the beginnings of dual inheritance theory, which is based on the notion that human behavior (and perhaps that of a small number of other species, like chimpanzees) has both genetic and cultural causes, and that culture, like genetics, is a system of inheritance. Subsequently dual-inheritance theory was developed in a string of journal articles and books (Boyd and Richerson, 1985; Cavalli-Sforza and Feldman, 1981; Durham, 1991; Pulliam and Dunford, 1980 for a small sample of these) all of which shared the assumption, sometimes explicitly stated but most often implicit, that the cultural component of dual-inheritance must be based upon certain key psychological mechanisms. This accords with what I will call Kitcher's rule that "without a serious psychological theory onto which the considerations about cultural transmission can be grafted" no understanding of culture by any natural science is possible (Kitcher, 1987, p. 95). The problem, though, is a mismatch between Kitcher's "serious psychological theory" and what dual-inheritance theorists have offered.

For Pulliam and Dunford, "observational learning is the basic mechanism by which information is culturally transmitted from generation to generation" (p. 57), innovative acceptance is a psychological issue of significance, as is the acquisition of behaviors that "increase pleasure, reduce pain, reduce anger, reduce fear or increase cognitive consistency" (p. 66). Cavalli-Sforza and Feldman laid stress upon "imprinting, conditioning, observation, imitation, or . . . direct teaching," while Boyd and Richerson, too, emphasized imitation and teaching. It is, of course, all too easy, as well as mean-spirited, to criticize serious biologists for playing amateur psychologists, especially as all were clearly adhering to Kitcher's rule. It nonetheless will not do to practice Kitcher's rule with an outmoded 1950s style of learning theory.

The most striking ommision from the psychological mechanisms advanced by dual-inheritance theorists is explicit reference to language. Absent also is reference to complex memory structures known variously as schemas, frames, scripts, and memory organization packets. There is also no mention of the wonderfully rich vein of knowledge that has emerged over the last couple of decades from the study of cognitive development of children relating to the understanding of physical and social causation, and the extent to which these are innate mechanisms which find cognitive expression through complex sequences of learning. That human cognition is rooted in human genes is surely of central concern to a group of theories that advance as their core notion some admixture of biological and cultural causation. It might be of some interest to historians of science that one of the most fiercely criticized, in some respects rightly so, attempts to biologize the study of culture, that of Lumsden and Wilson (1981), which was not a dual-inheritance theory, did consider this a key issue, and led them to develop the basis of a form of nativist cognitive development that chimes much better psychologically with contemporary cognitive psychology than anything offered by anyone else.

This brings us to a thread in this story upon which I rest most of my case. Running like a conceptual fault line through all of 20th century psychology is the struggle between empiricism and nativism, which sadly is still with us (see Quartz and Sejnowski, 1997, with accompanying commentaries for recent examples). In fact, Lorenz (1965), who incidently was recognized and lauded by Campbell at a time when it was not politically or intellectually correct to do so, had glimpsed a resolution to this age-old problem which has never received the recognition that it deserves. Lorenz understood that cognition of every form is itself a product, directly or indirectly, of evolution. There is no alternative view, of course, but the implications are enormous. Because every learner enters a world that is an unlabelled place that can be partitioned in a virtually infinitely large number of ways, in Edelman's (1987) phraseology, if learning is not to be a hopelessly slow and cumbersome process, a significant part of it must be pointed at those parts of the world that should be learned. In other words, cognition is, and must be, constrained, which Lorenz captured with his notion of "innate teaching mechanisms." This notion of constraint on cognitive adaptations long predated the later controversy and argument on how adaptations at large are to be regarded in terms of various sources of possible constraint. Some of these innate teaching mechanisms point human cognition to that part of the world that allows humans to enter into culture. In my view, it is extremely unlikely that human culture is dependent upon just one psychological or cognitive mechanism, and many of the cognitive mechanisms likely to be shown to be implicated are complex devices. Complexity is important here because for all our inability to find a metric for complexity in biology, and especially in psychology, most biologists buy into the general argument that the more complex a phenotypic feature is, the more likely it is a product of evolution by selection. If the human capacity for culture is dependent upon a number of psychological components, many of them complex, then we have linkage between human culture and human biological evolution. Culture is, somehow, the product of evolutionary processes and events. So, whatever these necessary, specific, cognitive constraints and psychological components are, if even only one of them has evolved, then the human capacity for entering into culture has evolved. And that gives us one particular route into understanding the relationship between evolution and social constructions because, as I will argue below, social constructions are at the heart of human culture.

The Essence of Human Culture

Hundreds of definitions of culture are available (Keesing, 1974; Kroeber and Kluckholm, 1952). The only way to deal with such conceptual profligacy is to choose one's meaning on the basis of the particular drum one wants to beat, provided that science can be done with it. With Kitcher's rule in mind, Goodenough's (1957) "culture consists of whatever it is one has to know or believe in order to operate in a manner acceptable to its members" is a good choice because it is amenable to analysis in terms of psychological mechanisms. Which mechanisms is an empirical matter, but a first theoretical throw at identifying them depends on what it is "one has to know or believe." The problem with the psychological mechanisms offered by dual-inheritance theorists to date is that they explicitly portray, or imply, a culture based upon shared knowledge of motor skills. That might be appropriate to protocultures in non-human species which may share skills to a limited extent (Whiten et al., 1999), and it might be appropriate to the earliest form of human culture, but it certainly is not appropriate for contemporary human cultures (Tomasello, 1999).

Human cultures can be considered in many different ways, even as many different things, as the plethora of definitions shows. The ideational approach of Goodenough argues that cultures are shared complex belief and knowledge systems which can result in physical structures and institutions outside of ourselves, but in the first instance the shared beliefs and understanding are products of interacting minds. As always, with something as complicated as culture, communication is greatly aided by example. So consider the example of justice, which in Western industrialized societies is based upon notions of fairness and ownership. This is not an inevitable and immutable outcome of human biochemistry. Other cultures regard justice differently, in terms of vengeance, kinship, priviledge of birth or service, or complex metaphysical metaphors. Justice will result in physical structures like law courts, bailiffs, and funny wigs. But the important feature of justice is that its "function cannot be performed solely in virtue of the sheer physical features of the phenomenon" (Searle, 1995, p. 228). Justice is not a building or some one person playing a particular role, such as a judge, or a collective of people like a jury. Justice is an agreement, hence Searle's "collective intentionality," between the members of a social group regarding how those individuals are to interact with one another. Justice is a social construction, and cultures are made up of large numbers of social constructions, amongst other things.

Thus, culture is not some invisible "culture stuff" that fills the air between the members of a social group; nor, from this point of view, is it the actions of individuals which may be the manifestation of culture; and nor is it the actual physical features of the world. Culture is what is shared in the minds of the members of a social group. One of the things shared is social constructions, which are things that exist only because we agree that they exist in the form that they do. Thus, other cultures will comprise individuals who share the agreement that justice has some other basis, and hence will have differently socially constructed notions of justice.

Used in this way, social constructions should not be confused with the way the phrase is used in the sociology of science debate (e.g., Woolgar, 1988). The existence of social constructions as defined here does not mean that the world is knowable only as a set of local, social phenomena. And while there are interesting connections to made with the ways sociologists use the phrase (Berger and Luckmann, 1967), as well as with the social-psychological notion of social representation (Moscovici, 1984), my concern here is with the psychological mechanisms underpinning agreed beliefs, be they about justice, money, marriage, patriotism, or any of the other myriad social constructions that make up any one culture.

Before speculating on what these mechanisms might be, a word is in order as to the causal reality of social constructions. Occasionally, natural scientists display a certain scepticism about social constructions, and doubt whether they are made of the same kind of stuff as the rest of us or can ever be encompassed within causal explanations. One answer to such doubters, it seems to me, is to point to how people live and die because of social constructions. Warfare is seldom the consequence of human aggressive instincts. It is mostly caused by patriotism, money markets, religion, ideologies, international treaties, and ethnic identities, all of them social constructions. Most people fight wars in a state of terror, not aggression, and have died in this way in many millions through human history. That is some causal force. As to whether they are the same stuff as hands or hearts, of course neural networks have the same material substance as muscle and bone. If social constructions are caused by interacting neural networks residing in separate brains, that just makes them complicated, not without material structure.

Candidate Psychological Components

Theorizing on this issue at present is not far from guess work. But on one guess there is unanimity. Language is essential to the existence of social constructions. The recognition of language as a uniquely rich and rapid extragenetic form of information transfer between individuals is widespread, and even described as one of the major transitions in the evolution of life on Earth comparable to, say, the evolution of multicellularity (Szathmary and Maynard Smith, 1995). The latter claim is based on the assumption that language is all that is necessary for culture, which is probably wrong. Nonetheless, the *central* role of language is surely correct and undisputed. What is contentious is how language is to be viewed in evolutionary terms, and when it first appeared. All possible positions have been taken on both issues, which is a fair measure of how little we know about the evolution of language. For this writer, all the evidence supports a strong nativist position. Language is also remarkably complex. For biologists, I believe without exception, anything that is both innate and complex in design is a consequence of evolution by selection. This applies to language as it does to all other complex psychological traits (Pinker, 1994; Plotkin, 1997). As for first appearance, views range from that of Tobias (1995) arguing for language in *Homo habilis* as long ago as two million years before the present to others (for example, Bickerton, 1995) who place its first appearance some time in the last 200,000 to 100,000 years. Some place it even later than that. The currently untestable truth is likely somewhere between these extremes since, contrary to one-gene saltationist theories of language (see Crow, 2000, for the most recent example), it is probable that language did not appear suddenly. Getting the anatomy of the throat and mouth right, as well as their innervation and control with hemispheric asymmetry and by appropriately sculpted neural networks that will generate rule-governed language required modification to a suite of genes, not some single mutation, and would have required a long period of time. How long is not known, but long enough surely for other features of human cognition and communication to have evolved alongside language. Mimesis (communication through mimed actions) and imitation are obvious candidates whose requirements for reference and the control of sequential, concatenated motor skills would have involved psychological mechanisms that might have been incorporated into an evolving language capacity. The evolution of hand gestures and skilled hand movement have also been implicated in language evolution (Corballis, 1999; Place, 2000).

Another cognitive module that might have evolved concurrently, or interleaving with, language is what is known as Theory of Mind, that is, the capacity to attribute intentional mental states to others. Indeed it is possible that the existence of language, mimesis, and imitation in some form, no matter how limited, were essential for the emergence of Theory of Mind in humans, and may still be a requirement of its normal ontogeny. The reverse position can also be argued. That is, language carries with it the intention to alter the mental states of others, and for this to be so, Theory of Mind is a necessary precursor to language. Whichever way it went, "interleaved" is likely the best description for what we know right now. However that may be, I suggest that a Theory of Mind mechanism is probably necessary for entering into an understanding of social constructions. Unlike the place of language, this is a much more tentative suggestion, based partly on my doubts that shared meaning of complex abstractions can be supported just by linguistic exchange. That social constructions are built on agreement and exist in the form that they do hints at the possibility that necessary to their maintenance is an understanding not just that others have intentional mental states, but that the contents of those states of mind are in some kind of matching relationship to one's own intentional states. I know of no direct evidence to support this view. But there is a literature on the development in children of a range of social constructions, including politics (Haste and Torney-Purta, 1992), money (Sevon and Werkstrom, 1989), courtesy (Song, Smetana, and Kim, 1987) and equity of reward (Hook and Cook, 1979). There is also a strongly held view that the cause of certain forms of childhood developmental disorders is a lack of the mechanisms that underpin Theory of Mind (e.g., Baron-Cohen, 1995). I am not aware of any study that has looked at the capacity for autists to incorporate social constructions, but this is one obvious empirical way forward.

I offer one further possible psychological mechanism, nicely illustrated by an intriguing study of Campbell himself (Jacobs and Campbell, 1961). In the 1930s, Muzafer Sherif used the autokinetic effect, which is the apparent movement of a fixated and stationary point of light in a darkened room, in a classic series of experiments which showed that when people are asked as a group to estimate the amount of apparent movement, estimates quickly stabilize around some shared norm. The formation of shared norms, Sherif asserted, is a fundamental feature of social living and occurs across a range of judgments and beliefs. The psychological mechanism(s) mediating the effect has been variously labeled conformity, obedience, and social cohesiveness. What Jacobs and Campbell did, using the autokinetic effect, was to set up a "rigged" social group in a darkened room comprising at the outset just one naive subject and a number of stooges instructed to give, when asked, absurdly overstated amounts of apparent movement of the light. The naive subject was asked to give his or her estimate last. Such was the extent of social force acting in this situation that the naive subjects always gave very much greater estimates of apparent movement than did individuals from a non-rigged control group. Then one stooge was removed from the group to be replaced by a second naive subject and the procedure was repeated until all the stooges had been replaced by naive subjects. The experimental group continued to give significantly higher estimates of apparent movement of the light, even when all the subjects in the experimental group were naive. This was a laboratory demonstration of the formation and maintenance of a cultural tradition in which social force biased the belief and judgment of a group of people—even though the judgment related to an illusion, which the subjects did not know.

Susceptibility to social force directly contributes, as Sherif originally argued, to agreement; it constitutes a kind of conceptual cement within which shared beliefs and judgments, including social constructions, are set. It is probably an evolved psychological trait selected for in a species about whose evolutionary history we can be certain in only one respect—life was lived in small social groups, the coordinated activity of which was probably significant to the survival of the individuals making up the group. While aquatic hypotheses, the necessity for cheater detector modules, the precedence of scavenging over hunting, and other speculative ideas about human evolution are and always will be just that, the likely existence of the small social group over a period of about seven million years is evidenced by the social behavior of contemporary hunter-gatherer peoples, as well as the social behavior of chimpanzees and gorillas, the two living ape species widely agreed on the basis of molecular genetic analyses to be the closest living relatives to *Homo*. It is unlikely that small social group living evolved independently in these species, or that while present in the common ancestral species, it was lost and then regained in the *Homo* lineage. This is the strength behind the recent attempt to reinstate the notion of group selection in human biology: "Since humans have lived in small groups throughout their history, it is reasonable to expect the evolution of psychological mechanisms that cause them easily to become 'team players' in competition with other groups" (Wilson and Sober, 1994, p. 601). Susceptibility to social force, I suggest, is one of these mechanisms.

In summary, whether through intensive and prolonged interaction between developing infants/children and their caretakers, more explicit and formal education, or the operation of brute social force, we establish agreed mental states and values on matters that relate in large part to the existence and continuing function of the social group, which, in turn, ensures the survival of individuals. I suggest that at a minimum, the extragenetic transmission of information, especially language, some elaboration on a theory of mind mechanism which allows for a matching of own to others' intentional states, and a responsiveness to social force, are the psychological mechanisms necessary for the evolution of the human capacity for social construction. These mechanisms are either not present at all, or only weakly so, in other species of great ape. They appeared sometime during the last six or seven million years, and like most other features of humans, they are products of evolution. In this sense, human culture is not different from our hands or our hearts. Extraordinary as culture is, and especially the social constructions that characterize it, it is the consequence of evolved organs of mind.

A Reservation

Anyone with a little knowledge of psychology and an elementary understanding of the complexities of human culture can only quail and quake at the size of the task of providing a psychological account of culture, since it could be argued to encompass the whole of psychological science with all its attendent controversies and unresolved questions. For example: why three mechanisms? Why not more? Why not less? This takes in the fraught issue of how many separable mechanisms and organs of mind there are. Just what is the structure of the mind? For example, is it possible that language and Theory of Mind are products of the same "theory generating" device, some single mechanism operating in different domains? There are no answers to these questions at present, which take in the deepest, the most fundamental questions there are to be asked about the mind. On the other hand, who said that applying Kitcher's rule was going to be easy? We just have to accept that given the tentative nature of psychological theory at present, a natural science of culture will be no less tentative. All that we can expect is that the two will advance together.

Other Ways, Other Questions

If culture has entitivity then we should be able to shake it down to its basic units which we can then describe and measure. This is the world of memes, the cultural analogues of genes. There is an awful lot of conceptual tidying up that needs to be done with the meme notion before it will have any use. This is not a new problem (Hull, 1982), but there has been little serious attempt to solve it. Whether social constructions are memes, for example, is simply a matter of taste. That, of course, is not good enough. So a further way of biologizing the social sciences is to try to make sense of memes by anchoring the idea to actual or potential empirically knowable features of our psychology. Right now it would seem that anything can be taken to be a meme, and to have some kind of equal weighting with other memes. So, to use a hoary old example from cognitive psychology, the schema for a restaurant as a place you go to, and in return for money, food will be prepared and brought to you, and you don't have to clean up after eating it, such a schema is a meme, but no different from the meme that Martha's Greasy Spoon around the corner serves a stunningly good English breakfast. This simply does not seem right, if for the only reason that the restuarant schema is a once-in-a-lifetime transmission event, whereas memes about specific examples of the schema can be transmitted every day, and many times each day, the difference being several orders of magnitude.

I have briefly suggested elsewhere (Plotkin, 1996) that memes might be ordered on the basis of cultural universality and rates of transmission. Thus, what might be called stem memes will be cultural universals, and the building blocks for all other memes. These are, in effect, psychological predispositions, such as entering into close affectional relationships with a small number of people, or attending to and dealing with features of small group living, like sharing and exchanging resources, entering into alliances, responding to strangers, and joining with mutual defence arrangements. Such predispositions are cashed out into culture-specific memes which, like genes, are transmitted at generational rates—we receive them, in the main, just once in a lifetime. For example, the use of money as a means of regulating the sharing of resources in some cultures, and the use of barter in others. Then there are the fleeting, rapidly transmitted and rapidly changing memes, surface memes, which are the froth of social life in any culture—this is a good restaurant, that is good grazing ground, he is untrustworthy, and she is kind and caring. There is, I suggest, an empirical program waiting to unfold here.

Part of Campbell's program was the development of a scheme within which could be fitted things both social and biological, and which allows for an understanding of the two-way causal interactions between the social and the biological—a device which, in effect, removes the conceptual barriers between them. Hence his notion of "downward causation" (Campbell, 1974a). Downward causation refers to the dynamic nature of control hierarchies, where information and causal power flow in all directions. Many social hierarchies are control hierarchies. Government is a control hierarchy writ large. The power of presidents and prime ministers is indeed great. However, public pressure and opinion exerts causal force on the decisions of our rulers, and when it does not, the rulers do not retain power for long. One way of envisaging the relationship between the biological and the social is that of a control hierarchy, comprising biological evolution, individual development, individual intelligence and cognition, and culture. The flow of causal interaction between them, specifically between biological evolution and culture, in some ways the stuff of gene-culture co-evolutionary or dual-inheritance theory, is another, as yet little explored and understood, way of casting social constructions as having entitivity. There are well-documented cases of cultural practices affecting human biology, lactose tolerance and animal husbandry being the classic example (Durham, 1991). Surely social constructions which have resulted in warfare and genocide must have altered gene frequencies and thus played a causal role in human evolution, just as have the use of fire and changes in diet altered human evolution. I can offer no hints as to how these be cast as science, but have no doubts about the general truth of the assertion that social constructions have been causal forces in human evolution. Now there is entitivity for you.

Concluding Comments

Culture is a "hyper-referential word" (Kuper, 1999). Materialist, adaptationist, ideationalist, structuralist, and symbolist schools of thought pursued this most human and complex phenomenon in a variety of ways through the 20th century. Mostly it was done within a strictly social science framework, with cultural anthropologists and sociologists fearful of the destruction that could be done by the oversimplifications threatened by biologists. Campbell favored an adaptationist view of culture in which it is a system for maintaining human survival in a variety of ecologies; and as a social psychologist, no one could have been more sensitive than he to the subtle complexities of culture. I have no doubt that he understood well the legitimacy of different approaches. In this chapter I have chosen to follow the line that the core characteristic of culture is that it comprises a sharing of something, indeed many things, between the people making up a social group, and have emphasized social constructions as one of the things shared because they are pervasive, powerful, and challenging. My general approach is that one way of naturalizing the study of culture is to chase down the psychological mechanisms that underpin the human capacity to enter into culture. This is not at all at odds with Campbell's adaptationist stance. He would have understood the complementarity perfectly.

8

Natural Tensions: Realism and Constructivism

LINNDA R. CAPORAEL

Naturalistic epistemology is pulled in opposite directions by two facts (Callebaut, 1993). One is the fact of Darwinism; the other is the social construction of facts. The first fact leads to realism; the second, in Donald Campbell's (1997) words, to "ontological nihilism." Campbell wanted neither. He rejected the lure of foundationalism, the attempt to provide an ultimate justification for true belief, and he insisted that nature participated as a co-referent in the selection of scientific theories. Nevertheless, Campbell thought of himself as both a Darwinist and a social constructivist.

Campbell envisioned a tension between biological evolution, which favored a genetic self-interest, and cultural evolution, which preached a group interest. The tension was repeated in his analysis of science, as one between the necessary social processes of science, which undermined competence of reference, and the norms of science, which accounted for whatever validity science might have. In this paper I use some of the tools that Campbell left us to develop a different understanding of the tensions between genes and culture, common knowing and scientific knowing, and sociality and cognition in his work. I propose that human cognition is fundamentally social cognition, a consequence of selection by functional social unit (Campbell, 1983b). One result is another tension, perhaps irresolvable, between responsiveness to contingencies in the habitat and the requirements for within group coordination.

This paper is divided into three sections. The first focuses on dualist tensions in Campbell's dark vision of human nature and its relationship to his theory of science. The second section describes a model for the evolution of human sociality drawing on Campbell's (1974a) critical concepts of downward causation and selection by functional social unit (Campbell, 1983b). The model is illustrated by revisiting Campbell's (1979b) tribal model of science and combining it with Hull's (1988a) demic structure of science. Where social constructivism is typically associated with recent trends in post-modernist thinking, the model I present suggests that *Homo sapiens* have always been social constructivists. The last section of the paper returns to Campbell and the sociologists and philosophers of science he called ontological nihilists. I suggest that for Campbell, the norms of science were also moral norms that preserved democratic values. In challenging these norms, the social constructivists offered no alternative set of values that could hold Campbell's Hobbesian world of genetic competitors in check.

Natural Tensions

Campbell sidestepped foundationalism by arguing that the "scandal of induction" was an unavoidable feature of perception. He also adopted, with qualification, Bradie's (1986) distinction between the evolutionary epistemology of mental mechanisms (EEM), concerned with the evolved cognitive abilities of humans (among other organisms), and the evolutionary epistemology of theories (EET), which applied Darwinism as an analogy to the problem of the fit between belief and referent. As Campbell himself realized, the distinction is not much of a barrier. While it is possible at one level to talk about EET as if humans were uninvolved ("the theory spread from France to England"), eventually questions arise about the minds and societies that enable the selective retention of some theories and not others.

Biology versus Culture

In early work, Campbell (1965b), like Darwin, posited a form of community selection. The many advantages to be had, including the "economy of cognition," would result in selection for an ambivalent human nature. Campbell believed that the complexity of the genetic system made it likely that there would be genetic variability in social-coordinative functions that would have been favored by natural selection. However, persuaded by G. C. Williams (1966) and William Hamilton (1964) on the fate of genetic altruism and by their arguments against group selection, Campbell recanted his earlier position (1975a, 1972). He embraced a narrow definition of "biological" as meaning DNA molecules (1983b); he reified genes as a form of unconscious psychology, and for a social constructionist he was surprisingly unsuspicious about producing "a [sociobiological] portrait of human nature compatible with traditional religious, literary, sociological and psychological views . . ." (1983b, p. 37). For a man who gave and received so much affection, generosity, and good will, Campbell had a rather dim view of minds and societies. He was a nature-nurture dualist, and to him "biological" human nature was fundamentally selfish, barely held in check by cultural preaching for the common good. Societies were fragile coalitions based on cooperation among genetic competitors, where the strong ". . . forc[ed] altruism on group members who cannot survive without cooperative group membership . . ." (Campbell, 1983b, p. 37).

Campbell's touchstone for human evolution and the source of major tensions in his work became "cooperation among genetic competitors." He saw biological evolution as "ending" with the face-to-face group, with cultural evolution picking up where the face-to-face group left off. Distinguishing between two forms of selection, biological and cultural, he reworked his earlier view of an ambivalent human nature as an antagonism between self-interest and societal sanctions. His paper "On the Conflicts between Biological and Social Evolution and between Psychology and Moral Tradition" vividly pictured the tensions as a spring, anchored at one end by biological selfishness and at the other end by social system preaching (Campbell, 1975a).

Epistemological Tensions

In his discussion of genetic competitors, Campbell seemed to be assuming an urban society of faceless aggregates of individuals. Other work is concerned with face-to-face groups, where the picture is more complex. For example, his notion of "clique selfishness" (Campbell, 1982b) stresses within group coercion and cooperation at the expense of larger collective interests. To a large extent, Campbell separated these "social dispositions" from cognitive mechanisms. In presumably smaller groups, he stresses cognitive interdependence (e.g., Jacobs and Campbell, 1961). Some of the interdependence is a function of collective competence—the idea that several observers should have a more valid perception than would a single observer. Another force for interdependence is the reliance we must place in others for our knowledge of the world. He speculated that humans would evolve a meta-rationality for consensus over validity when the two were in conflict that would undermine the goal of truth because collective action could be more adaptive than individualistic action or no action at all (Campbell, 1990c).

However, Campbell preferred to keep these speculations separate from his concerns with a selection theory of science. According to Campbell, science "supposes itself to operate in a different ecology than did our neohuman tribes" (1990c, p. 46). Mental mechanisms arose through biological evolution, but scientific theories were a product of cultural evolution. Campbell's concern was that a focus on mental mechanisms would lead to an evolutionary foundationalism for epistemology, which Campbell thoroughly rejected (Campbell, 1990b).

Working primarily from the example of perception, Campbell argued that our cognitive mechanisms could not provide justification for realism because they were "presumptive all the way down."

Although Campbell disdained the cognitive mechanisms, the social dispositions were crucial to his epistemology (Campbell, 1997). He saw the scientific community as a necessary "vehicle" of knowledge. However, it was far from perfect. The social processes of science operated against the discovery of valid knowledge. Scientists were no different from other human communities identified by their practices, beliefs, ideologies, and in-group loyalties. To the extent that science could claim higher validity than other belief systems, it would be because within its belief system it incorporated "anti-tribal" social norms. These norms, including disagreement based on evidence, resistance to tradition, and a view of truth lying in the future, enabled nature to participate as a co-selector of belief. Campbell's central argument is that if we assumed that science did produce more valid beliefs than did alternative social systems, it would be because of its anti-traditional norms.

In the previous paragraphs, I have argued that Campbell had a dark vision of human nature, separated into social dispositions and cognitive capabilities. These led to a prescriptive position to preserve those norms at high cost because they did allow nature to participate in the discovery of truth. In the section to follow, I propose that Campbell left tools to build a different model of human nature. Without doubt, it bears his influence, but it replaces the dualisms between good and evil, between cultural preachings and genetic impulses, and between cognition and sociality.

Tools

As Campbell recanted his 1965 paper defending the evolution of altruism, he made a case for *downward causation*, arguing that "where natural selection operates through life and death at a higher level of organisation, the laws of the higher-level selective system determine in part the distribution of lower-level events and substances" (Campbell, 1974a, p. 180). He subscribed to familiar reductionist principles: that all levels of organization conformed to the constraints imposed by lower levels, including those from physics, and that explanations at higher levels required specifying lower-level mechanisms and processes. But Campbell denied that reductionism could constitute a complete explanation. There were laws of organization that could not be reduced to physics or inorganic chemistry. The shape of a soldier ant's jaw, for example, was an emergent biological phenomena that could not be explained only in terms of subatomic particles. If there were differential replication at higher levels of organization, then the distribution of lower-level "events and substances" would be partially determined by selection at the higher level. That is, lower-level substances, including genes, would be sorted and not selected (c.f., Vrba, 1986).[1]

"Downward causation" was written as a side discussion for a conference in 1972, and I suspect that Campbell himself failed to recognize its implications until rather late in his career (Campbell, 1990a, 1994a, 1997). Nevertheless, it became an early and influential contribution to an emerging hierarchical or multi-level selection theory (Brandon, 1990; Buss, 1987; Gould, 1980; Sober and Wilson, 1998; Wilson and Sober, 1994). Instead of competition between selfish genes or even genetic competitors, multi-level selection theory posits a hierarchy of levels of selection, populated by different entities, including macromolecules, genes, cell lineages, individuals, and even groups. This view of evolution provides a radical departure from the more familiar genocentric approaches common in evolutionary epistemology and psychology. It trades the moral overtones of selfish genes and cultural altruism for a discussion focused on *coordination* within and between levels of organization (Buss, 1987). It also emphasizes the functional relations that evolve between entity and environment, de-emphasizing "genes for" organismic traits.

In later years, Campbell did come to see the implications of downward causation and multi-level selection theory for bringing development into an evolutionary framework. Structural relations between entity and environment vary over the life history of organisms with consequences for replication in the succeeding generation. Campbell (1990a) wanted "to see *every* level of organization within the organism as being achieved in development and kept in order by a node of selection" (p. 19, emphasis in original). Through processes of downward causation, epigenetic factors at different levels organize genetic activity, and in many cases must be present for phenotypic development. Such reliable presence argues against privileging the gene as the sole unit of heredity; it also argues for expanding notions of heritability. For evolution and for development to occur, genes, higher level entities, resources at various levels or organization, and all the relationships among these components must come together, at the right time and place, generation to generation (Caporael and Baron, 1997).

One notable item that humans and their ancestors have repeatedly assembled is face-to-face group living. Campbell (1994a, 1982b, 1975a, 1983b) argued that adaptations for sociality could arise through selection by "functional social group." As proto-humans came together for protection from predation and other benefits of group living, a feed-forward ratcheting process would be put in motion. The result would be the evolution of social dispositions such as mutual monitoring, moralistic aggression to outgroups, and clique selfishness.

Campbell's argument can be expanded. To the extent that exploiting a habitat is more successful as a collective group process than as an individual process, not only would more successful groups persist, but so also would individuals better adapted to group living (Caporael et al., 1989). Selection by functioning social unit would lead to truly *social* groups as opposed to aggregates of individuals. Truly social groups are like bodies (which are entities at a lower level or organization) in that they have structural requirements including internal differentiation of tasks and roles, organization of individual efforts, communication, and boundary definition (Brewer, 1997). Thus, the key issues for an evolutionary perspective on groups—and social behavior generally—are the achievements and failures of coordination.

Although Campbell believed in genetic self-interest, he left tools for constructing a view of evolution and evolutionary psychology that went beyond the tension of selfish genes and moralizing culture. By helping to lay the framework for multi-level evolutionary theory he opened the possibility for seeing culture as every bit as crucial to the formation of human phenotypes as are genes. His idea of selection by functional social group leads the way in seeing how human psychology is shaped by interactions among humans.

Naturalizing Social Constructivism

Core Configurations

Elsewhere I have hypothesized a model of the nested structure of face-to-face groups (1997, 1995; Caporael and Baron, 1997). The basic idea is that human cognition is adapted to a small number of core configurations. These are based on the size of a nested subgroup and recurrent features of tasks for which the configuration is particularly well-suited. Size/task configurations are repeatedly assembled generation to generation as a functional consequence of the physical relation between morphology and ecology. To illustrate such relations, consider the number of people who can simultaneously examine an object held in the palm of one's hand compared to the number of people who can hold a baby or the number who can gather round to hear a tale. In these cases, the recurrent relations between morphology and ecology can be thought of as niches that afford (but do not guarantee) the evolution of correlated cognitive processes. For example, dyads afford possibilities for *micro-coordination* (e.g., facial imitation in a mother-infant dyad, the automatic adjustment of gait that occurs when two people walk together, etc.). A group of four to five people affords possibilities for *distributed cognition* (the sharing of memory, perception, contextual cues, etc.); a group of about 30 people affords culture, but not reproduction, which requires a "group of groups" an order of magnitude larger for sufficient genetic variability in sexual reproduction. This larger group also affords the standardization and stabilization of language (and knowledge) over a broad area.

The next section illustrates some features of the core configuration model by comparing some size/task configurations among hunter-gatherers to those among scientists. It also suggests a continuity of social cognitive processes despite the dramatic differences in culture.

Scientists and Foragers

Campbell is well known for his work on the "tribal structure of science" (Campbell, 1979b, 1997). By tribal structure, Campbell referred to the social processes (e.g., in-group loyalties) that make science a self-perpetuating community. In his view, these processes were required to sustain science as a knowledge-carrying community, yet they are antagonistic to competence of reference. However, if the processes required to sustain science are social *cognitive processes*, they may also be *necessary* to whatever competence of reference exists.

Campbell's description of a "tribal" structure to science, rather than, say, a market structure or bureaucratic structure (to which science is now turning), was especially insightful. There are parallels between the typical organization of nomadic hunter-gatherer groups (Jarvenpa and Brumbach, 1988) and of scientists (Hull, 1988a). Hull's (1988a) work is particularly important in this regard, and the following discussion draws heavily on it.

Both scientists and hunter-gatherers have a nested hierarchy composed of work groups (research groups), bands (primary face-to-face groups), and seasonal macrobands (tribes). In both instances—in science and among hunter-gatherers—group-size numbers at these levels are fairly constant; groups of about three to five individuals (hunters or lab research groups), 30–50 individuals (bands, conceptual demes, or primary social groups), and 300–500 individuals (tribes of hunter-gatherers and of scientists) (Birdsell, 1972; Hassan, 1981; Hull, 1988a). If we add the dyad, we have four repeatedly assembling configurations: dyad, work group, "bands," and "tribes" (Caporael, 1997).[2] The following is a brief sketch of the parallels between group organization and functional activities.

In some sense, both hunter-gatherers and scientists work in the (hypothetically) "real world." Hunter-gatherers must find resources for survival; scientists search for explanations of phenomena in the world. Scientists and hunter-gatherers have a variety of techniques directed, with considerable effort, to reducing the unpredictability and uncertainty of their experience. In both instances, isolated individuals have reduced viability. Individuals must be part of a subgroup with sufficient "critical mass" to persist. Isolated hunter-gatherers are vulnerable to many dangers; isolated scientists are not very productive. Similar to hunter-gatherer groups, which reproduce by fission, scientists do not usually begin a new research group as social isolates; they must bring some of the old group members with them or attract new recruits.

Similarities of function also exist in the subgroup configuration structure of scientists and hunter-gatherers. Learning to fashion specialized tools, in stone or other materials, or to use specialized laboratory techniques or "primitive" food preparation techniques, is a hands-on, situated activity (like golf or tennis). Such learning requires feedback from materials, equipment, and an experienced mentor if novices are to develop finely tuned sensory-motor micro-coordination. Frequently this learning takes place in dyadic interactions, not unlike the parent-child interaction through which children learn shared reference in language by ostension (Campbell and Paller, 1989).

For both lab groups and small hunter-gatherer groups, ambiguity is a major attribute of the task environment. Hunters must detect an animal equipped with natural camouflage and distinguish predator from prey, gatherers must distinguish toxic from nourishing plants, and scientists in the lab must detect the signal in their data from the noise. Yet solitary humans seem poorly equipped for this task: the correlation between two "theory-free" co-variates must reach the vicinity of .8 before it is detected (Nisbett and Ross, 1980). In some sense, seeing, as opposed to perception, may be viewed as a group process. In their investigations of scientists in the lab, Amann and Knorr-Cetina (1990) proposed that "processes of seeing appear to be interactionally dissolved in shop talk" (p. 115). Thus, the "machinery of seeing" ambiguous data (autoradiograph film) is talk. What scientists seem to do is to build group-level "pattern detectors." Small groups of four or five people can distribute cognition; they share tasks such as perception, classification, inference, memory, and contextually cued responses when they interpret data or interact with uncertain features in the habitat.

In hunter-gatherer workgroups, food from the hunt is often brought back to the domestic base and shared in the band. Bands are the basic functional economic unit, and operate for the processing and maintenance of resources and information retrieved from the smaller dispersed groups (Jarvenpa and Brumbach, 1988). Scientists bring their research results and interpretation to workshops and small conferences of their "conceptual demes." Bands/demes afford a shared construction of reality ("common knowledge"), some of which may be mythical, some of which may be acutely attuned to local conditions, from detailed knowledge of other people to the local ecology. They are also the staging ground for cooperative alliances, which are the basis for fissioning when the community exceeds resources or is fractured by conflict.

The traditional hunter-gatherer macroband is a seasonal collection of bands, generally related by common origin stories, customs, ritual, and most enduringly, language. Language not only holds together a common worldview, which in turn enables highly coordinated behavior, it also allows the sharing of important information about distant locales. For language to serve this function, it must be stable (a word or phrase refers, most of the time, to the same thing) and standard (the word or phrase must be understood within a community of users). Similarly, scientists have their yearly conventions where they learn about developments farther afield, but possibly relevant to their own concerns, and where new terminology and procedures are introduced and debated. For both scientists and hunter-gatherers, seasonal meetings (or yearly conventions) are important for the exchange of myths, gossip, and information. They are also arenas for competitive games as well as the affirmation of common worldviews, the maintenance of languages (hunter-gatherers) and specialized professional terms (scientists), and the exchange of people (mates, new Ph.D.s, or disgruntled members).

Evolutionary Social Epistemology

It should be clear by now that this paper is more closely aligned with social epistemology (Fuller, 1991; Thagard, 1994), which is not particularly evolutionary, than it is with evolutionary epistemology (Kornblith, 1985; Wuketits, 1990), which is not particularly social. Traditionally, evolutionary epistemologists have looked to perception to ground evolutionary justifications for realism: "[A]ny process that has at its center a bloody struggle for existence must necessarily commit one to a fairly robust sense of the reality of things" (Ruse, 1990, p. 101). This appeal to evolutionary realism might apply to solitary living creatures that are directly adapted to conditions of the habitat (if we dispute the presumptiveness of the senses). The human case is more complex. It is true that we can usually negotiate a room full of furniture using our visual system. Such perceptual acuity is a primate adaptation, effectively evolved long before the appearance of humans and their immediate ancestors. But as Amann and Knorr-Cetina's (1990) work suggests, perception is not necessarily the same as seeing. What human groups add to perception is resolving power through artifacts that embody knowledge, cross-generational extension of memory, and potential error correction. In one sense, adaptation to the social group undermines the "direct" access to the environment many realists assume; in another sense, the closest access to the real is what can be socially seen. If the model sketched above is approximately correct, then uniquely human cognition is fundamentally social cognition, the result of two different levels of selection, individual and group.

The model of core configurations and the parallels between foragers and scientists is a devilish suggestion that social constructivism evolved. Knowing is an ineluctably social process. The world is socially constructed in two related senses, as distributed cognition and as shared realities. In small workgroups, cognition is functionally distributed and externalized. It is the product of dynamic interaction with the social and material world and a division of cognitive labor. In their study of "transactive memory," Liang, Moreland, and Argote compared individuals who trained together on a technical task to individuals who were individually trained and then performed the task in newly formed groups (1995). Groups trained together outperformed individuals who were trained separately. They also had better recall about the technical procedures, and there was specialization within the group for remembering distinct aspects of the procedures and higher trust in each other's knowledge. This kind of cognition is *situated*. It takes place in small face-to-face groups where perception, perspective, and memory are distributed through talk across group members and artifacts to achieve specific, concrete tasks.

In contrast, certain aspects of shared reality are *unsituated*, such as some beliefs and attitudes. Demes and macrodemes reproduce, stabilize, and standardize collective identity and shared worldviews or paradigms that organize (and are organized by) the activities at lower levels of organization. Where distributed cognition is situated by tasks that give it form and structure, shared realities function as unsituated filters on experience. For some peoples, the stars in the sky are holes in the floor of heaven; for others, they are gaseous balls of flame. While the perception of pinpoints of light in a dark sky are the same, the seeing of the stimuli is different. These worldviews act as an interpretive filter; they are the background assumptions that inform individual experience and the coordination of work in workgroups and demes. Freyd (1983) has argued that knowledge, and the cognitive and linguistic structures we assume for it, is constrained by "shareability." She predicts that a new term has to fit existing components of shared reality to be successfully introduced into language. Moreover, attempts to introduce new terms will be subverted by taking on meanings in the direction of prior knowledge.

There is, of course, no guarantee that social cognition will regularly produce more valid beliefs than individuals. Some evidence indicates that subjects *in groups* presented with an ambiguous stimulus quickly come to a shared perception of the stimulus, but the perception is dead wrong (Jacobs and Campbell, 1961; Sherif, 1935). Human seeing is also theory-driven. Just as people underperceive objective correlations, they overperceive low or non-existent correlations if they have a theory suggesting a relationship (Nisbett and Ross, 1980). However the lack of a theory can be just as problematic: parts of the natural world under investigation may not even be "see-able." For example, Hull (1988a) describes Pearl's and Root-Bernstein's experiments inspired by Mendel's suspicious pea data. Both found that in the absence of pre-established character states, neither trained scientists nor naive undergraduates were able to classify two varieties of maize on two different characters: there were too many intermediates and the result was idiosyncratic classifications. *With* a description of the character states, the classification results were similar to Mendel's (and too good to be true).

The parallels between hunter-gatherers and scientists seem to suggest no genuine demarcation between science and other belief systems. Campbell invoked the anti-tribal scientific norms of science to explain its success. However, many areas of inquiry have similar norms, including law and some areas in the humanities (Barzun and Graf, 1992). Moreover, the case can be made that many of science's most notable achievements may require the demic structure of science, complete with tribal norms (Griffith and Mullins, 1972). Tribally normative background assumptions are essential for stabilizing the interpretation of data. This is not to say that traditional scientific norms are irrelevant, but that it may be equally important to look at the historical development of the heuristic practices of science. Many such practices (e.g., the use of control groups) may be the product of trial-and-error in the cultural evolution of knowledge-making.

Doubtless the success of Western science is the result of numerous factors. One that is likely to be ignored, and does differentiate hunter-gatherer communities from scientific communities, is the elimination of anthropomorphism. This may not seem to be an important factor if one assumes an asocial cognition, or, as is typically done, assumes that only children and "savages" anthropomorphize. However, if cognition is fundamentally social, we expect humans to attribute human characteristics to phenomena that are otherwise inexplicable yet important to human goals or outcomes (Caporael, 1986; Caporael and Heyes, 1997; Humphrey, 1976). Precisely because of the underdetermination of explanation, it is essential that invisible spirits be rejected on an *a priori* basis if material causes are to have a chance of being co-referents in the selection of belief.

In terms of a naturalistic epistemology, this view of human cognition suggests a multi-level selection process with conflicts and synergisms among different levels of organization. The tension between realism and constructivism may be more than a conflict between two different philosophical positions. Instead, it may be built into our bodies and minds. We should expect a tension—or at best an uneasy compromise—between responsiveness to contingencies in the environment necessary for survival (realism) and the requirements for within-group coordination, also necessary for survival (social constructivism). The tension leaves us with a dilemma. If humans have evolved as social constructivists, there may be no transcendental "human nature," but only historical sequences of descriptive paradigms, of which genetic competition and sociality are two, comparable more in their generativity than in their truth value.

Campbell and the Social Constructivists

Campbell was fond of talking about his "relativist friends" and his "ontological nihilist friends," and his affection was genuine despite their differences. He used a quote from Collins (1981a) to characterize their position: "[The research results show that] the natural world has a small or nonexistent role in the construction of scientific knowledge" (p. 3). It was a position that Campbell was completely unwilling to accept. The other irreconcilable difference was Campbell's conviction that science was a more adequate social institution for producing better approximations to truth than could other social institutions. Campbell (1997) allowed that there might be a certain excess in the social constructivists' claims. "[S]ince they were all pressed by the need to write brief, vivid, and publishable books and articles, in which only one-tenth of their notes could be used, a postresearch selection bias in the 'constructed out of whole cloth' direction is possible" (p. 35). But having admitted this, he continued focusing on the "excess."

Characteristically, Campbell described himself as a selective "winnower" in contrast to the social constructivists—he held up the sociologist Sal Restivo as a "wildman." But as Restivo and Croissant point out (1995; Restivo, in press), there were no ontological nihilists among the thinkers Campbell engaged. Knorr-Cetina describes herself as an ontological realist (Callebaut, 1993); Bloor (1976) and Collins (1985) defend science as the best available form of inquiry; and with a hint of exasperation, Latour (1988) suggested that a little relativism is a good thing, but too much relativism sends one back to realism. Campbell ignored these qualifications. He respected and agreed with much the social constructivists had to say (Campbell, 1986a): "I identify my own position as completely 'constructivist' and go on to posit fallibly that to some degree the social winnowing processes characterizing science lead to the selective propagation of those few social constructions that refer more competently to their presumed ontological referents" (p. 512).

For one who so much valued better approximations to truth and objectivity, Campbell's identification of the social constructivists as ontological nihilists was strangely provocative.[3] Restivo (in press) points out that Campbell had far more in common with them than he admitted. Even stranger was that Campbell (1997) urged hypocritically preaching the anti-tribal norms of science. By hypocrisy, he meant that the ideals of science should be preached, even if they were mostly honored in the breach. These norms included neutrality, absolute honesty with data, the agreement to disagree, status in the community predicated solely on scientific merit, and even a commitment to "facts that speak for themselves." For a lover of truth, even if it was at best an approximation, Campbell's championing of hypocrisy seems perplexing.

I think the contradiction can be explained. Campbell saw humans as biologically selfish, a state which he compared to the religious version of original sin (1976, 1983b). Even if social systems preached absolute, self-sacrificial, altruistic behavior, such preaching would fail to bring a society to the biosocial optimum between self-interest and group interest. He trusted the social processes of science as a vehicle for belief change much more than he trusted government, religion, or cultural evolution in general (Campbell, 1986a). I believe that Campbell saw the traditional "anti-traditional" norms of science as more than scientific norms; they were also moral norms.

The parallel is evident in Campbell's (1990c) paper honoring the psychologist Solomon Asch. Asch is best known for his research on "conformity." In these studies, subjects in a group were presented with slides of lines of various lengths, and one at a time, announced which line was the longest. In actuality, there was only one subject in the group; the others were confederates of the experimenter. On some trials, the first "subjects" announced that the second longest line was the longest, even though it was patently shorter than the longest. A third of Asch's subjects conformed to the confederate majority. Campbell argued that these studies should be reinterpreted in view of the dependence we have on others for knowledge. Accordingly, the Asch studies should be seen as a structural conflict between the respect we have for each other's reports (trust) and our duty to report our observations honestly (honesty). Campbell believed that the subject faced a dilemma. If honesty prevails, the subject reports the line is shorter and fails in trusting. If trust prevails, the subject completes the consensus of the group but fails in honesty and self-respect (our duty to integrate our own and others' reports "without deprecating them or ourselves," p. 46). The "epistemological moral imperatives" Campbell saw in Asch's work were also imperatives in his own views: trust, honesty, and self-respect.

Campbell and his wife, the anthropologist Barbara Frankel, passionately held egalitarian, anti-authoritarian values. They rejected personal power or charisma as arbiters of truth and they disapproved of privilege in any domain. For a while, Campbell even advocated "fair start capitalism," a 100 percent inheritance tax that would prohibit passing money from one generation to the next and help fund education for the poor comparable to that received by children of the wealthy. (His enthusiasm waned on hearing that some people would deny themselves comforts in their later years or perhaps even die in penury so that their children might inherit. This was for him another moral complication that needed a resolution.)

Although Campbell did not explicitly use the word "democracy," the overlap between scientific and democratic values appears in his description of the tribal model of science (Campbell, 1988e). He poses a set of queries where the lines between the two are smudged: Is not science less authoritarian (than churches or the military)? Less likely to squeeze out the insubordinate young geniuses? More likely to promote them at an early age? Less likely to engage in favoritism? Compared to the humanities and social sciences, less likely to be influenced by prejudices of the external society? To have faculty members on the Social Register? Writes Campbell, "These values of science I want to keep alive and available for use in the arguments that are made in the course of *institutional* decision making. These values will, I believe, make a difference—a difference in favor of truth" (1988e, p. 500, emphasis added).

These are passionate words, almost a plea to the social constructivists. My interpretation is that Campbell saw more than just the justificatory claims of science at stake; that in pulling the curtain away from the Wizard of Science and exposing its vulnerabilities, the social constructivists undermined the anti-tribal norms. However, they failed to put in place new alternatives. In Campbell's Hobbesian world of genetic competitors, held together by altruistic preaching, the social constructivists threatened not just science, but the social order that sustained it.

In the end, I think that Campbell had less confidence in scientists than he would have liked because he had so little confidence in our species. This may have been related to his own history (Campbell, 1981a). He was not only of another generation, with service in WWII, but also his experience as a scientist was drawn from another realm. Where most of the social constructivists were originally trained as natural scientists and engineers, Campbell began his career studying ethnocentrism and racial prejudice. In graduate school in California he collected data on children and young people's attitudes toward Jews, Negroes, Japanese, Mexicans, and out-groups in general. His dissertation, a separate project, measured social distance, blaming, capability, morality, and affection toward the same groups. The results of this work were never published, but one can imagine that in the 1940s, there would be little in the data to encourage optimism.

Campbell's background may help us understand why he took such a dim view of human nature, and perhaps even why he even used the inflammatory term "hypocrisy." We know that there are normative systems that are far from perfect, such as the oxymoron of "just war." However, preaching the ideals of just war and training the young to take honor in serving those ideals saves far more lives in war than would be saved in the absence of such rules. Similarly, preaching the ideals of science should produce less fraud, less error, and more valid understanding than if those ideals were not preached. There are, I believe, important differences between the failure to achieve overly idealistic goals and hypocrisy, the latter edged as it is with cynicism. For those who knew Donald Campbell, therein lies a mystery, because he was far from cynical or hypocritical. He was a dedicated scientist and scholar, convinced that better approximations to the truth were always possible and worth striving for.

My view of human nature is not so dark as Campbell's, and I believe that the anti-tribal norms of science can be stretched to accommodate the most important findings of the social constructionists as well as a different vision of human motivation and capacities. Perhaps with greater awareness of human interdependence, expanded scientific norms might be forged. These would recommend humility in the face of the unknown, an appreciation of the social and political context of science, a critical stance within scientific communities, and a generosity of spirit across disciplinary boundaries—all norms embodied in the life and work of Don Campbell.

Notes

I am indebted to Marilynn Brewer and Sal Restivo, who, living at the opposite ends of Don Campbell's conceptual territory, helped me work through the last section of this paper. I hope they meet someday. I am grateful to Barbara Frankel, who kindly heard me out and gave me the details of "fair start capitalism"; to Harry Collins for his view of his notorious quote about the minimal role of the natural world in science; and to the editors, Cecelia Heyes and David Hull. As usual, Glen Culbertson and John Schumacher made numerous helpful suggestions, and as usual, I was headstrong, so there is only me to blame for the errors.

1. Campbell (1990) was well aware that his emergentist principle and downward causation would have to be "settled judgments of plausibility in the arena of contingent, descriptive statements, and not logical proof" (p. 4).

2. In Caporael (1997) I used a terminology based on demes to denote a broader generality than the anthropologist's language of bands. In biology, deme refers to a breeding group. The word derives from the Greek term *demos* and refers to a political unit defined by geography rather than kin ties. My debt to David Hull (1988a), for recognizing the demic structure of science, should be obvious.

3. Of course, one might wonder by what accidents of fate or wrong-headed misreadings that these realists became so notorious as social constructionists.

9

In Search of Epistemological Warrant

DAVID L. HULL

The Cazenovia Conference

Although I had met Donald Campbell briefly through the years, I did not get to know him well until he invited me to a conference at Lake Cazenovia near Syracuse University in the spring of 1981. Campbell had noticed with some trepidation that those of us who studied science had become increasingly factionalized. Philosophers, historians, and sociologists of science had never been all that tolerant of each other to begin with. Philosophers were bright enough, but they tended to take an extremely cavalier attitude toward the history of science and spent most of their time arguing issues of no possible interest to anyone else, including scientists. Historians, for their part, were certainly careful. They partitioned off a small area of science and made it their own. If nothing else, historians of science supplied philosophers with examples they could use in their more abstruse endeavors. Sociologists of science were still largely Mertonian in outlook (Storer, 1973). Perhaps the Puritans did not play quite the role in the origin of Western science that Merton claimed, but his basic functionalist norms of science seemed appropriate enough.

But starting in the second half of the 1970s, new approaches to science studies exploded—Barry Barnes's (1974) Sociology of Scientific Knowledge, David Bloor's (1976) Strong Programme, Bruno Latour and Steve Woolgar's (1979) ethnographic study of laboratory life, Harry Collins's (1981b) Radical Programme and much, much more. All sorts of methodologies that had their origins in literary criticism, rhetoric, comparative literature, and French philosophy were vying for dominance in this increasingly contentious literature. More traditional philosophers looked at these upstarts with haughty condescension. When social constructivists said that scientists construct facts, did they really mean that scientists make up what they claim to be facts out of whole cloth? Did these young upstarts have to rediscover every philosophical wheel and march down every blind alley? Were they really as ill-educated as they seemed? For their part, traditional historians were aghast at what passed for scholarship in this literature. Just when historians of science had come to see that no historical event or sequence of events can be explained in terms of one or two sorts of causal factors, these young Turks declared that everything can, and must, be explained in terms of social causes, e.g., class status, sexism, racism, and homophobia.

As dismayed as more traditional philosophers and historians were by this plethora of nonstandard methodologies invading their territories, Mertonian sociologists of science were the main targets of these polemics. At times, radical critics of Mertonian norms argued that they did not characterize science at all. Instead of scientists rerunning every experiment before they use its results, they usually just accept the work of other scientists without testing it. How unscientific can you get? At other times, they presented a more measured view. For example, Collins (1982, p. 301) admits that "academic science exhibits more universalism, communism, disinterestedness, and scepticism than other professional institutions, though not nearly enough."

Campbell was alarmed by all the discord that accompanied the introduction of so many different perspectives into science studies, each group claiming hegemony. If only representatives of these various schools could sit down in relative quiet and discuss these issues, we would discover common ground and might even produce a synthesis of some sort. Toward this end, Campbell organized the Cazenovia conference. The acronym for the subject matter of this conference was ERISS: Epistemologically Relevant Internalist Sociology of Science. At the time, "internalist" sociology of science meant traditional sociology of science in terms of those factors that are internal to science, such as organized skepticism in contrast to such external factors as gender or social class. Campbell hoped to show that internalist sociology of science is epistemologically relevant, i.e., organizing science and scientists in certain ways increases the credibility of the results produced.

As I recall, Richard Boyd presented a paper early in the proceedings that reaffirmed to many at the conference the commonly held caricature of "positivist" philosophy of science. Boyd set out traditional formalist philosophy of science with all the care that he could muster. Perhaps if these crazies could be made to understand some basic positions in the philosophy of science, they would stop talking such nonsense. Those participants who were not raised in traditional philosophy were far from amused. Steve Woolgar was also one of the early speakers. He simply read a transcript of a conversation among scientists. Periodically, someone in the audience interrupted him, suggesting a message to be learned from this transcript, some point to it. Do men interrupt women more often than women interrupt men? Perhaps this transcript illustrated how ineffectual arguments are in the conduct of science. I chirped up, "Are you going to argue that?" The meeting went down hill from there.

Campbell's Evolutionary Epistemology

Donald Campbell is justifiably considered the father, possibly the grandfather, of evolutionary epistemology. He is commonly viewed as reasoning by analogy from the adaptive fit between organisms and their environments brought about by gene-based selection in biological contexts to the legitimacy of all sorts of beliefs, including those held by scientists. One goal of this paper is to show that this widely held interpretation of Campbell's views is mistaken. (Happily, the authors of the papers in this volume do not perpetuate this misunderstanding.) Instead, from the start, Campbell argued for a general selection theory. Gene-based biological evolution is one instance of this general sort of process, the reaction of the immune system to antigens is another instance, social learning is yet another, and so on. None of these instances has any priority over any of the others. The epistemological warrant comes from Campbell's general selection theory, not any one instance of this general kind. However, in a paper published posthumously by Cecilia Heyes and Barbara Frankel, Campbell (1997) rejects the preceding view as well. His general selection theory does not provide any epistemological warrant either. Whatever validity science has comes from the social structure of science (Campbell and Paller, 1989). This social structure, in turn, is a combination of orthodox Mertonian sociology of science and "symmetrical, relativist, social constructivist, sociology of scientific belief" (Campbell, 1997, p. 13).

So many people have studied Campbell's work and so much has been written about it that any widespread misunderstanding of his fundamental principles seems unlikely, but misunderstanding there is. He is widely held as emphasizing a strong analogy between gene-based selection in biological evolution and other forms of selection such as sociocultural evolution. For example, in his most influential publication, Campbell (1974b, p. 413) asserts that evolutionary epistemology is "at minimum an epistemology taking cognizance of and compatible with man's stature as a product of biological and social evolution." In numerous places Campbell (1965a, p. 26) expresses himself in ways that encourage the view that he was offering an "analogy between natural selection in biological evolution and the selective propagation of cultural forms." But he goes on to explain that the "analogy to cultural cumulations will not be from organic evolution *per se*, but rather from a general model for adaptive fit or quasiteleological processes for which organic evolution is but one instance."

The paradigm example of a selection process is gene-based biological evolution. Biological evolution is "gene-based" in two senses. The only variations that matter are those that get passed on in the genetic material. In addition, certain characteristics are in some sense "programmed into our genes." Some of us have the "gene for blue eyes." Massive sustained criticisms have been lodged against the preceding ways of expressing both genetic replication and the complex relationship between genes, environment, and the resulting phenotype. So, it is objected, genes all by themselves are incapable of replication. A very complex cellular apparatus is also required. In addition, the gene for blue eyes does not determine eye color all by itself. Numerous other factors are involved. Perhaps discussions in terms of codes, information, programming, and the like can be misleading at times, but I know of no alternative terminology that works any better. Certainly, a total rehash of beginning genetics cannot be introduced every time one mentions either transcription or translation.

If we accept that species evolve the way that evolutionary biologists think that they do, then organisms should be reasonably well-adapted to their environments. Once again, unrelenting criticism is lodged about referring to "adaptations." Regardless of the impression that outsiders might get from reading the popular literature on Panglossian adaptationism, professional biologists expend considerable effort in providing well-founded adaptive scenarios. For example, little genuine doubt remains about the origin and maintenance of the alleles responsible for sickle cell anemia. Allelic differences produce differences in phenotype. Of course, some slippage exists in gene-based selection. No features of organisms are perfectly adapted. Good enough has to be good enough. And environments do change. At one time a particular feature of an organism may have been reasonably well-adapted to its environment, but in the meantime the environment has changed. Now it is amazingly maladaptive.

Such overly studied criticisms to one side, biologists maintain that behavioral traits (such as the tendency to hide rather than explore when presented with a new environment) can be selected for just as readily as ordinary phenotypic traits (such as the tendency to put on weight, or remain thin no matter how much one eats). Although the literature on the possibility of explaining behavioral and sociocultural traits on the basis of gene-based selection in strictly biological contexts is huge, Campbell himself sees no problems on this score. Some behavioral and sociocultural traits are programmed into our genes in the same way as are ordinary phenotypic traits. However, sociocultural traits have a second avenue of transmission as well—social transmission. Much of individual and social learning cannot be explained in terms of a direct application of evolutionary theory as a biological theory. Instead it has to be explained analogically. Much of what we know is not programmed into our genes but programmed into our brains. Such knowledge is passed on socially, not genetically.

From the beginning, Campbell was clear that his "evolutionary epistemology" was actually the subsumption of various sorts of selection processes under his general selection theory, not reasoning by analogy from gene-based selection to other forms of selection. Even so, he was aware that selection in biological evolution is the most secure and well-worked out example of selection. Reasoning from analogy at the very least is a productive heuristic. As Campbell (1959, p. 170) notes, "The evolutionary analogy may lead us to see a justification for certain trends in science as a social system which we might otherwise judge as unworthy." For example, biological evolution is opportunistic. No one is tempted to chastise this natural process for exhibiting such an unseemly characteristic, but as Einstein noted, scientists are also extremely opportunistic. If biological evolution proceeds so successfully through opportunism, then perhaps we should withhold judgment with respect to the behavior of scientists. Perhaps opportunism in science is also a virtue.

Campbell's General Selection Theory

The periodic use that Campbell makes of the analogy between gene-based selection in biology and other sorts of evolution gives the impression that he thinks that biological evolution is somehow more fundamental than other forms of selection. It is, but only because we happen to know more about it than we do of any of the other examples of selection, but the immune system is catching up fast. Soon, we will have two well-worked out unproblematic examples of selection. But, from his earliest publications, Campbell (1956b, 1959, 1960) emphasized that he was attempting to apply a general account of selection to a variety of processes, *not* reasoning by analogy from selection in biological evolution to other examples of selection. In the application of a general selection theory to a variety of processes, selection in biological evolution loses its special status. It is just one more example of a selection process.

Although Campbell (1997, p. 13) changed his mind over the years on a variety of subjects, his epistemological interests remained undiminished:

> My own agenda for the past thirty-five years has been to relate the philosophers' epistemological problems to evolutionary theory, and to that more abstract model of discovery and adaptation shared by trial-and-error learning, natural selection, cultural evolution, acquired immunity, radar, sonar, echolocation, and vision: "selection theory" for short.

The question then becomes whether or not such a general selection theory can provide epistemological warrant. Most professional epistemologists have never been all that impressed by Campbell's naturalistic, evolutionary epistemology, in part because it is naturalistic, but at least they could appreciate the strength of the analogical reasoning from biological to sociocultural evolution. However, Campbell's general selection theory is supposed to be the source of epistemological justification. Gene-based selection can be subsumed under this general selection theory, but so can the reaction of immune systems to antigens, trial-and-error learning, and a host of other phenomena. The question then becomes the warrant that such subsumptions afford. Campbell (1965a, p. 27) argues that, given the conditions necessary for selection to occur, an "evolution in the direction of better fit to the selective system becomes inevitable." Certainly one might *explain* one sort of selection by subsuming it under a more general characterization. After all, such subsumptive explanations were once thought of as paradigm explanations. But Campbell is after epistemological warrant, not subsumptive explanation. If Campbell is taken as arguing analogically from biological to conceptual evolution, then he can claim at least some limited warrant for applications of evolutionary epistemology—though not the sort of warrant that would satisfy very many philosophers. To the contrary, if Campbell is taken as arguing for the subsumption strategy, then he can claim no warrant at all.

The arguments against both evolutionary epistemology in the narrow sense of reasoning by analogy and Campbell's general selection theory are familiar. Adaptation does not guarantee truth. Holding false beliefs can be more advantageous in the struggle for survival and reproduction than beliefs that are closer to the truth. Apparently, human beings are strongly predisposed genetically to view the living world in terms of stereotypes, but this predisposition cannot be used to argue against evolutionary theory. Viewing biological species in this overly simple way may be sufficiently advantageous in the struggle for existence and reproduction to result in its continued prevalence in the human species, but even so, species are genetically quite variable, and variation is at the heart of any selection process. Most beliefs have little in the way of a genetic contribution, but the same conclusion follows. For example, believing that God is on your side is very advantageous in times of war. An army made up of reasonable people who can see both sides of the conflict is not likely to survive for long. When the most decorated soldier in World War II was asked what made for a good soldier, he replied, "Youth and ignorance."

Lots of slippage exists in gene-based selection. One cannot expect social learning to be perfect either. It does not have to guarantee truth in all instances. An occasional mistake can occur. The trouble is that in certain instances selection leads to systematic errors. Widespread false beliefs are frequently quite advantageous. The issue is not that "truth" and "successful" are conceptually distinct but that the two are frequently not even highly correlated. For a long time the preceding argument did not persuade Campbell, but in the decade before his death, he had concluded that even subsumption under his general selection theory did not provide epistemological warrant:

> When the evolutionary model came to be used in more detail to describe general principles in the history of scientific theory transmission, change, and especially speciation (as by Toulmin, 1967, 1972; Richards, 1981, 1987; Hull, 1982, 1986) the epistemological agenda has been almost entirely lost. (Campbell and Paller, 1989, p. 242)
>
> The many efforts to model the "evolution" of scientific knowledge on the principles of biological evolution (e.g., Toulmin, 1967, 1972; Richards, 1981, 1987; Hull, 1982, 1986, 1988a, 1988b) I now judge to be epistemologically irrelevant. (Campbell 1997, p. 8; see also 1987b, p. 151)

In the preceding declaration Campbell may be rejecting analogies between biological evolution and the evolution of scientific knowledge, but the authors whom he lists share Campbell's non-analogical view of evolutionary epistemology. All three adopt the subsumptive strategy. Hence, Campbell should have put his own name on the list. Toulmin, Richards, Hull, and Campbell all attempted to explain the evolution of scientific knowledge by subsuming it under a general selection theory. Even Sir Karl Popper might well have held the subsumptive position (Hull, 1999, p. 487).

However, just because the selective character of science as a process is epistemologically irrelevant, it does not follow that selection cannot be invoked to explain quite a bit about science. I, for one, never thought that my general analysis of selection as applied to science had any epistemological relevance at all. In fact, I angered more than one of my philosophical colleagues by stating that the fault with evolutionary epistemology lies not with its being evolutionary but with its being epistemology. All the effort that Campbell and others have put into what has been called misleadingly "evolutionary epistemology" is certainly worthwhile. It is just not "epistemology," not even naturalized epistemology.

Sociology of Scientific Validity

Campbell is not about to give up the search for epistemological warrant. If his general selection theory does not justify the fit between scientific theories and their subject matter, then something else must. This something else turns out to be the social structure of science. In 1987 Campbell published a paper entitled "Selection Theory and the Sociology of Scientific Validity," and the title of Campbell's 1997 posthumous paper is "From Evolutionary Epistemology Via Selection Theory to a Sociology of Scientific Validity." Whatever validity scientific knowledge claims might have stems not from its arising by means of a selection process but from the social structure of science.

However, there are social structures and social structures. The social system of mutual citation, exchanging credit for use, and so on, that I set out for science (Hull, 1988a) applies just as well to numerous other groups, including religious sects. Campbell's (1997, p. 151–2) own "insight came from the fact that the variation-selection-reproduction-speciation-genealogy model applied equally well to the Appalachian Bible-belt free churches in which my grandfather, uncle, and cousins participated." In his posthumous paper, Campbell (1997, p. 9) concluded that beliefs about normal middle-sized objects and events which vision produces are "justified" by two separate plausiblities. The first is the old familiar one: organisms that had eyes which mislead them too seriously were weeded out. The result is eyes that can be trusted, except . . . and here a whole series of provisos are assumed. The second justification concerns "co-selection by objects of belief" (Campbell 1997, p. 9). The referents of beliefs play a crucial part in their selection. A common belief is that barking dogs do not bite. As you approach a barking dog, you put this belief to the test. One religious sect includes as part of its religious services the handling of venomous snakes, such as rattle snakes. They believe that they will not be bitten but, if bitten, they will not be affected.

Campbell goes on to emphasize that beliefs are also co-selected by a host of factors that detract from their validity.

Scientists are organized to some extent along the lines of Merton's norms, but they must also do all the things necessary to maintain their groups, to obtain funding, etc. They are also influenced by all sorts of interests and historical constraints that have little to do with these Mertonian norms. For co-selection to offer sufficient justification, it must overwhelm all the other co-selectors. Thus, the internalists are right that co-selection by the objects and events of our beliefs influence these beliefs. The externalists are right that all sorts of other co-selectors are also operative. Certain social conventions that are present in science are largely absent in the case of the snake handlers. One contribution that those scholars who advocate a symmetrical, social constructivist, sociology of scientific beliefs is to bring home time and again how influential such externalist co-selectors actually are. Of course, these later workers decline to call these co-selectors "external" because they think that they are just as internal to science as are Mertonian norms.

Conclusion

One major impression that I got from reading a lifetime of Campbell's publications on evolutionary epistemology is how long and hard he struggled to legitimize these views. He did change his position, only very slowly and with great difficulty. In his early work, he was willing to call any and all adaptive forms that result from genetic selection "knowledge." When that convention proved an impediment to various scholars, most noticeably philosophers, Campbell adopted a more traditional terminology. When he was convinced, after twenty years of struggle, that his general selection theory on its own could not provide epistemological validity, he altered the direction of his search for scientific validity to the social structure of science. Included in this social structure are requirements about testing views and taking the results of these tests seriously—which does not mean the instant abandonment of one's favorite hypothesis because one experiment seems to count against it (see chapter 13 in Hull, 1988a, devoted entirely to conceptual interaction).

I began this paper with a discussion of a conference held in Cazenovia in 1981 which Campbell hoped would decrease the agonistic aggression so common in science studies. He ended his posthumous paper with:

> . . . yet another plea to the social constructivists in sociology of science. I do so as part of my long-term effort to persuade them to entertain the possibility, however remote it might appear to them, that the real world might play a role in selecting the beliefs we come to have about it. If so, it follows that scientific discoveries may not be made up entirely out of the whole cloth. (Campbell 1997, p. 34)

As the recent Science Wars indicate, almost twenty years later plenty of ill feelings remain. According to Campbell (1997, p. 12), a selectionist model for justifying scientific beliefs depends on "the way the world is." He admits that spelling this out will lead to rather "orthodox" conclusions. For example, "experimentation is important." Campbell was willing to modify his views through the years but not so much as to make them vacuous. Perhaps if treating sciences as one more instance of selection does not supply warrant to the claims scientists make, the social structure of science—no matter how imperfectly captured by Merton's norms—does.

How well will Campbell's posthumous views sit with the various advocates of various versions of symmetrical, relativist, social constructivist sociology of scientific belief? One good sign is that many of the most influential contributors to this extremely heterogeneous literature are now claiming that they have been seriously misunderstood. They never held any of the interesting views for which they are famous. For example, in response to Alan Sokal's bad joke, Stanley Fish (1996) responded:

> What sociologists of science say is that of course the world is real and independent of our observations but that accounts of the world are produced by observers and are

> therefore relative to their capacities, education, training, etc. It is not the world or its properties but the vocabularies in which terms we know them that are socially constructed. (p. 23)

Thus, the claim that facts are socially constructed means only that the language in which the fact is expressed is socially constructed. The fact itself is not. But isn't this what Boyd was arguing years before at the Cazenovia conference? Of course, language is constructed. What else could it be? Even an evil positivist would accede to this uncontroversial claim. The latest cycle of realism and relativism has run its course. However, this cycle is not a circle. All sides now hold views that are at least slightly different from those with which they began. The war is over. All sides can declare victory and go home (see also Barnes, Bloor and Henry, 1996, and Caporael this volume).

References

Almond, G., M. Chodorow, and R. H. Pearce. 1982. *Progress and its Discontents*. Berkeley: University of California Press.

Amann, K., and K. Knorr-Cetina. 1990. The fixation of visual evidence. In *Representation in Scientific Practice*, edited by M. Lynch. Cambridge, Mass.: MIT Press.

Ashby, W. R. 1952. *Design for a Brain*. New York: Wiley.

Baldwin, J. M. 1909. *Darwin and the Humanities*. Baltimore, Md.: Review.

Baron-Cohen, S. 1995. *Mindblindness: An Essay on Autism and Theory of Mind.* Cambridge, Mass.: MIT Press.

Barnes, B. 1974. *Scientific Knowledge and Sociological Theory*. London: Routledge & Kegan Paul.

———. 1982. *T. S. Kuhn and Social Science.* New York: Columbia University Press.

Barnes, B., D. Bloor, and J. Henry. 1996. *Scientific Knowledge: A Sociological Analysis*. Chicago: University of Chicago Press.

Barzun, J., and H. F. Graf. 1992. *The Modern Researcher*. 5th ed. New York: Harcourt Brace Jovanovich.

Berger, P. L., and T. Luckmann. 1967. *The Social Construction of Reality.* London: Penguin.

Bickerton, D. 1995. *Language and Human Behavior.* Seattle: University of Washington Press.

Birdsell, J. B. 1972. *An Introduction to the New Physical Anthropology*. Chicago: Rand McNally.

Bloor, D. 1976. *Knowledge and Social Imagery*. London: Routledge & Kegan Paul.

Bourdieu, P. 1991. The peculiar history of scientific reason. *Sociological Forum* 5: 3–26.

Bowler, P. 1984. *Evolution: The History of an Idea*. Berkeley: University of California Press.

———. 1988. *The non-Darwinian Revolution: Reinterpreting a Historical Myth*. Baltimore: Johns Hopkins University Press.

———. 1996. *Life's Splendid Drama*. Chicago: University of Chicago Press.

Boyd, R. and P. Richerson. 1985. *Culture and the Evolutionary Process*. Chicago: University of Chicago Press.

Bradie, M. 1986. Assessing evolutionary epistemology. *Biology and Philosophy* 1: 401–459.

———. 1989. Evolutionary epistemology as naturalized epistemology. In *Issues in Evolutionary Epistemology*, edited by K. Hahlweg and C. A. Hooker, 393–412. Albany: State University of New York Press.

———. 1994. Epistemology from an evolutionary point of view. In *Conceptual Issues in Evolutionary Biology*, edited by E. Sober, 453–475. Cambridge, Mass.: MIT Press.

———. 1997. Quine as an evolutionary epistemologist. *Epistemologica* 20: 175–210.

Brandon, R. N. 1990. *Adaptation and environment*. Princeton: Princeton University Press.

Brewer, M. B. 1997. On the social origins of human nature. In *The Message of Social Psychology*, edited by C. McGarty and A. Haslam. Oxford: Blackwell.

Brewer, M. B. and B. E. Collins. 1988. *Scientific Enquiry and the Social Sciences*. San Francisco: Jossey-Bass.

Burchfield, J. D. 1974. Darwin and the dilemma of geological time. *Isis* 65: 300–331.

———. 1975. *Lord Kelvin and the Age of the Earth*. New York: Science History Publications.

Burkhardt, R. W. 1977. *The Spirit of System: Lamarck and Evolutionary Biology*. Cambridge, Mass.: Harvard University Press.

Bury, J. B. [1920] 1924. *The Idea of Progress: An Inquiry into its Origin and Growth*. London: MacMillan.

Buss, L. W. 1987. *The Evolution of Individuality*. Princeton: Princeton University Press.

Cain, J. A. 1993. Common problems and cooperative solutions: organizational activity in evolutionary studies 1936–1947. *Isis* 84: 1–25.

———. 1994. Ernst Mayr as community architect: launching the Society for the Study of Evolution and the journal Evolution. *Biology and Philosophy* 9(3): 387–428.

Callebaut, W. 1993. *Taking the Naturalistic Turn, or, How Real Philosophy of Science is Done*. Chicago: University of Chicago Press.

Calvin, W. H. 1987. The Brain as a Darwin Machine. *Nature* 330: 33–34.

———. 1990. *The Cerebral Symphony: Seashore Reflections on the Nature of Consciousness*. New York: Bantam.

———. 1996a. *The Cerebral Code: Thinking a Thought in the Mosaics of the Mind*. Cambridge, Mass.: MIT Press.

———. 1996b. *How Brains Think: Evolving Intelligence, Then and Now*. New York: Basic Books.

Campbell, D. T. 1956a. Adaptive behavior from random response. *Behavioral Science* 1(2): 105–110.

———. 1956b. Perception as substitute trial and error. *Psychological Review* 63(5): 331–342.

———. 1958. Common fate, similarity, and other indices of the status of aggregates of persons as social entities. *Behavioral Science* 3: 14–25.

———. 1959. Methodological suggestions from a comparative psychology of knowledge processes. *Inquiry* 2: 152–182.

———. 1960. Blind variation and selective retention in creative thought as in other knowledge processes. *Psychological Review* 67: 380–400.

———. 1965a. Variation and selective retention in socio-cultural evolution. In *Social Change in Developing Areas: A Reinterpretation of Evolutionary Theory*, edited by H. R. Barringer, G. I. Blanksten and R. W. Mack. Cambridge, Mass.: Schenkman.

———. 1965b. Ethnocentric and other altruistic motives. In *Nebraska Symposium on Motivation,* edited by D. Levine. Lincoln, Nebr.: University of Nebraska Press.

———. 1966. Pattern matching as an essential in distal knowing. In *The Psychology of Egon Brunswick*, edited by K. R. Hammond, 81–106. New York: Holt, Rinehart & Winston.

———. 1969. Ethnocentrism of disciplines and the fish-scale model of omniscience. In *Interdisciplinary Relationships in the Social Sciences*, edited by M. Sherif and C. W. Sherif, 328–348. Hawthorne, N.Y.: Aldine.

———. 1970. Natural selection as an epistemological model. In *A Handbook of Method in Cultural Anthropology,* edited by R. Narroll and R. Cohen. New York: Natural History Press.

———. 1972. On the genetics of altruism and the counterhedonic components in human culture. *Journal of Social Issues* 28(3): 21–37.

———. 1973. Ostensive instances and entitativity in language learning. In *Unity Through Diversity: A Festschrift for Ludwig von Bertalanffy*, edited by W. Gray and N. D. Rizzo. New York: Gordon & Breach.

———. 1974a. "Downward causation" in hierarchically organized biological systems. In *Studies in the Philosophy of Biology,* edited by F. J. Ayala and T. Dobzhansky. London: Macmillan.

———. 1974b. Evolutionary epistemology. In *The philosophy of Karl Popper*, edited by P. A. Schilpp. La Salle, Ill.: Open Court.

———. 1974c. Unjustified variation and selective retention in scientific discovery. In *Studies in the Philosophy of Biology*, edited by F. J. Ayala and T. Dobzhansky, 139–161. London: Macmillan.

———. 1975a. On the conflicts between biological and social evolution and between psychology and moral tradition. *American Psychologist* 30: 1103–1126.

———. 1975b. On the conflicts between social and biological evolution and the concept of original sin. *Zygon* 10: 234–249.

———. 1977. Descriptive epistemology. Unpublished William James Lectures, given at Harvard University.

———. 1979a. Comments on the sociobiology of ethics and moralizing. *Behavioral Science* 24: 37–45.

———. 1979b. A tribal model of the social system vehicle carrying scientific knowledge. *Knowledge* 2: 181–201.

———. 1981a. Another perspective on a scholarly career. In *Scientific Inquiry and the Social Sciences: A Volume in honor of Donald T. Campbell*, edited by M. B. Brewer and B. E. Collins, 454–486. San Francisco: Jossey-Bass.

———. 1981b. Levels of organization, selection, and information storage in biological and social evolution. *The Behavioral and Brain Sciences* 2: 236–237.

———. 1981c. Variation and selective retention theories of sociocultural evolution. *Current Anthropology* 22: 603–608.

———. 1982a. The "blind-variation-and-selective-retention" theme. In *The Cognitive-Developmental Psychology of James Mark Baldwin: Current Theory and Research in Genetic Epistemology*, edited by J. M. Broughton and D. J. Freeman-Moir, 87–97. Norwood, N.J.: Ablex.

———. 1982b. Legal and primary-group social controls. *Journal of Social and Biological Structures* 5: 431–438.

———. 1983a. The general algorithm for adaptation in learning, evolution, and perception. *The Behavioral and Brain Sciences* 6: 178–179.

———. 1983b. The two distinct routes beyond kin selection to ultrasociality: Implications for the humanities and social sciences. In *The Nature of Prosocial Development*, edited by D. L. Bridgeman. New York: Academic Press.

———. 1984. Toward an epistemologically relevant sociology of science. *Science, Technology and Human Values* 10: 38–48.

———. 1986a. Science's social system of validity-enhancing collective belief change and the problems of the social sciences. In *Metatheory in Social Science: Pluralisms and Subjectivities*, edited by D. W. Fiske and R. A. Shweder, 108–135. Chicago: University of Chicago Press.

———. 1986b. Science policy from a naturalistic sociological epistemology. In *PSA* 1984, vol. 2, edited by P. Kitcher and P. D. Asquith, 14–29. East Lansing, Mich.: Philosophy of Science Association.

———. 1987a. Neurological embodiments of belief and the gaps in the fit of phenomena to noumena. In *Naturalistic Epistemology: A Symposium of Two Decades,* edited by A. Shimony and D. Nails, 165–192. Dordrecht: D. Reidel.

———. 1987b. Selection theory and the sociology of scientific validity. In *Evolutionary Epistemology*, edited by W. Callebaut and R. Pinxton, 139–158. Dordrecht: D. Reidel.

———. 1988a. Perspective on a scholarly career. In *Methodology and Epistemology for Social Science*, edited by E. S. Overman, 1–26. Chicago: University of Chicago Press.

———. 1988b. Descriptive epistemology: Psychological, sociological, and evolutionary. In *Methodology and Epistemology for Social Science*, edited by E. S. Overman, 435–486. Chicago: University of Chicago Press.

———. 1988c. Fragments of the fragile history of psychological epistemology and theory of science. In *Psychology of Science,* edited by B. Gholson, W. R. Shadish and A. C. Houts. Cambridge: Cambridge University Press.

———. 1988d. A general selection theory, as implemented in biological evolution and in social belief transmission with modification in science. *Biology and Philosophy* 3: 171–177.

———. 1988e. *Methodology and Epistemology for Social Science*, edited by E. S. Overman. Chicago: University of Chicago Press.

———. 1988f. Popper and selection theory. *Social Epistemology* 2(4): 371–377.

———. 1990a. Levels of organization, downward causation, and the selection-theory approach to evolutionary epistemology. In *Scientific Methodology in the Study of Mind: Evolutionary Epistemology*, edited by E. G. Tobach. Hillsdale, N.J.: Lawrence Erlbaum.

———. 1990b. Epistemological roles for selection theory. In *Evolution, Cognition, and Realism*, edited by N. Rescher. Lanham, Md.: University Press of America.

———. 1990c. Asch's moral epistemology for socially shared knowledge. In *The Legacy of Solomon Asch*, edited by I. Rock. Hillsdale, N.J.: Lawrence Erlbaum.

———. 1993. Plausible coselection of belief by referent: All the objectivity that is possible. *Perspectives on Science* 1: 88–108.

———. 1994a. How individual and face-to-face group selection undermine firm selection in organizational evolution. In *Evolutionary Dynamics of Organizations*, edited by J. A. C. Baum and J. V. Singh. New York: Oxford University Press.

———. 1994b. Toward a sociology of scientific validity. In *Explaining Scientific Consensus*, edited by K. M. Kim, ix–xviii. New York: Guildford Press.

———. 1997. From evolutionary epistemology via selection theory to a sociology of scientific validity. *Evolution and Cognition* 3: 5–38.

Campbell, D. T. and G. A. Cziko. 1990. Comprehensive evolutionary epistemology bibliography. In *Evolutionary Epistemology: A Multiparadigm Program*, edited by W. Callebaut and R. Pinxten, 405–431. Dordrecht: D. Reidel.

Campbell, D. T., B. Holzner, and M. Shahidullah. 1985. Introduction: The comparative study of science and the sociology of scientific validity. *Knowledge: Creation, Diffusion, Utilization* 6(4): 307–328.

Campbell, D. T., and B. T. Paller. 1989. Extending evolutionary epistemology to "justifying" scientific beliefs (A sociological rapprochement with a fallibilist perceptual foundationalism?). In *Issues in Evolutionary Epistemology*, edited by K. Hahlweg and C. A. Hooker, 231–257. Albany: State University of New York Press.

Campbell, D. T., and J. C. Stanley. 1966. *Experimental and Quasi-experimental Designs for Research*. Chicago: Rand McNally.

Caporael, L. R. 1986. Anthropomorphism and mechanomorphism: Two faces of the human machine. *Computers in Human Behavior* 2: 215–234.

———. 1995. Sociality: Coordinating bodies, minds and groups. *Psycoloquy* (vol. 6, no. 01) [on-line serial]. Available from ftp.princeton.edu/pub/harnad/psycoloquy/1995.volume 6/;INTERNET.

———. 1997. The evolution of truly social cognition: The core configurations model. *Personality and Social Psychology Review* 1: 276–298.

Caporael, L. R., and R. M. Baron. 1997. Groups as the mind's natural environment. In *Evolutionary Social Psychology*, edited by J. Simpson and D. Kenrick. Hillsdale, N.J.: Lawrence Erlbaum.

Caporael, L. R., R. M. Dawes, J. M. Orbell, A. J. C. van de Kragt. 1989. Selfishness examined: Cooperation in the absence of egoistic incentives. *Behavioral and Brain Sciences* 12: 683–739.

Caporael, L. R., and C. M. Heyes. 1997. Why anthropomorphize? Folk psychology and other stories. In *Anthropomorphism, Anecdotes and Animals*, edited by R. W. Mitchell, N. Thompson and L. Miles. Albany: State University of New York Press.

Cavalli-Sforza, L. L., and M. W. Feldman. 1981. *Cultural Transmission and Evolution: A Quantitative Approach.* Princeton: Princeton University Press.

Chambers, R. 1853. *Vestiges of the Natural History of Creation.* 10th ed. London: J. Churchill.

Coleman, W. 1964. *Georges Cuvier Zoologist: A Study in the History of Evolution Theory.* Cambridge, Mass.: Harvard University Press.

Collins, H. M. 1981a. Stages in the empirical program of relativism. *Social Studies of Science* 11: 3–11.

———. 1981b. What is TRASP? The radical programme as a methodological imperative. *Philosophy of the Social Sciences* 11: 215–224.

———. 1982. Knowledge, norms and rules in the sociology of science. *Social Studies of Science* 12: 299–309.

———. 1985. *Changing order: Replication and Induction in Scientific Practice.* Beverly Hills: Sage.

Cook, T. D., and D. T. Campbell. 1979. *Quasi-Experimentation: Design and Analysis Issues*. Boston: Houghton-Mifflin.

Corballis, M. C. 1999. The gestural origins of language. *American Scientist* 87: 138–145.

Crow, T. J. 2000. Did *Homo sapiens* speciate on the Y chromosome? (vol. 11, no. 001) [on-line serial]. Available from ftp.princeton.edu/pub/harnad/psycoloquy/2000.volume.11/;INTERNET.

Cuvier, G. 1813. *Essay on the Theory of the Earth*. Translated by R. Kerr. Edinburgh: W. Blackwood.

Cziko, G. 1995. *Without Miracles: Universal Selection Theory and the Second Darwinian Revolution*. Cambridge, Mass.: MIT Press.

Darwin, C. 1859. *On the Origin of Species*. London: John Murray.

Darwin, E. 1789. *The Botanic Garden* (pt. 2, *The Loves of the Plants*). London: J. Johnson.

———. 1791. *The Botanic Garden* (pt. 1, *The Economy of Vegetation*). London: J. Johnson.

———. 1794–1796. *Zoonomia; or, The Laws of Organic Life*. London: J. Johnson.

Dawkins, R. 1986. *The Blind Watchmaker*. New York: Norton.

Deacon, T. W. 1997. *The Symbolic Species: The Co-evolution of Language and the Brain*. New York: Norton.

Desmond, A. 1994. *Huxley, the Devil's Disciple*. London: Michael Joseph.

———. 1997. *Huxley, Evolution's High Priest*. London: Michael Joseph.

Dobzhansky, T. 1937. *Genetics and the Origin of Species*. New York: Columbia University Press.

———. 1967. *The Biology of Ultimate Concern*. New York: The New American Library.

Durham, W. H. 1991. *Coevolution: Genes, Culture and Human Diversity*. Stanford: Stanford University Press.

Eccles, J. C. 1989. *The Evolution of the Brain: Creation of the Self*. London: Routledge.

Edelman, G. M. 1987. *Neural Darwinism: The Theory of Neuronal Group Selection*. New York: Basic Books.

———. 1988. *Topobiology: An Introduction to Molecular Embryology*. New York: Basic Books.

———. 1989. *Remembering the Present: A Biological Theory of Consciousness*. New York: Basic Books.

———. 1992. *Bright Air, Brilliant Fire: On the Matter of the Mind*. New York: Basic Books.

Eldredge, N., and S. J. Gould. 1972. Punctuated equilibria: An alternative to phyletic gradualism. In *Models in Paleobiology*, edited by T. J. M. Schopf, 82–115. San Francisco: Freeman, Cooper.

Eysenck, H. J. 1993. Creativity and personality: Suggestions for a theory. *Psychological Inquiry* 4: 147–178.

———. 1994. Creativity and personality: Word associations, origence, and psychoticism. *Creativity Research Journal* 7: 209–216.

———. 1995. *Genius: The Natural History of Creativity*. Cambridge: Cambridge University Press.

Finke, R. A., T. B. Ward, and S. M. Smith. 1992. *Creative Cognition: Theory, Research, and Applications*. Cambridge, Mass.: MIT Press.

Fish, S. 1996. Professor Sokal's Bad Joke. *The New York Times* Op-Ed, May 21.

Fisher, R. A. 1930. *The Genetical Theory of Natural Selection*. Oxford: Oxford University Press.

Fogel, L. J., A. J. Owens, and M. J. Walsh. 1996. *Artificial Intelligence Through Simulated Evolution*. New York: Wiley.

Ford, E. B. 1964. *Ecological Genetics*. London: Methuen.

Freyd, J. 1983. Shareability: The social psychology of epistemology. *Cognitive Science* 7: 191–210.

Fuller, S. 1991. *Social epistemology*. Bloomington, Ind.: Indiana University Press.

Giere, R. N. 1983. Testing theoretical hypotheses. In *Testing Scientific Theories*, edited by J. Earman, 269–298. Minnesota

Studies in the Philosophy of Science, vol. 10. Minneapolis: University of Minnesota Press.

———. 1988. *Explaining Science: A Cognitive Approach*. Chicago: University of Chicago Press.

———. 1989. Scientific rationality as instrumental rationality. *Studies in History and Philosophy of Science* 20: 377–384.

———. 1990. Evolutionary models of science. In *Evolution, Cognition, and Realism,* edited by N. Rescher. Lanham, Md.: University Press of America.

———. 1995. Science without laws of nature. In *Laws of Nature: Essays on the Philosophical, Scientific and Historical Dimensions*, edited by F. Weinert, 120–138. New York: Walter de Gruyter.

———. 1999. *Science without Laws*. Chicago: University of Chicago Press.

Goodenough, W. H. 1957. Cultural anthropology and linguistics. *Language and Linguistics* 9, edited by P. Garin, 167–173.

Gould, S. J. 1980. Is a new and general theory of evolution emerging? *Paleobiology* 6: 119–130.

———. 1981. *The Mismeasure of Man*. New York: Norton.

Greenough, W. T., and J. E. Black. 1992. Induction of brain structure by experience. *Developmental Behavioral Neurosciences* 25, edited by M. Gunnar and C. Nelson. Hillsdale, N.J.: Erlbaum.

Griffith, B. C., and N. C. Mullins. 1972. Coherent social groups in scientific change. *Science* 177: 959–964.

Gross, P. R., and N. Levitt. 1994. *Higher Superstition: The Academic Left and its Quarrels with Science*. Baltimore: Johns Hopkins University Press.

Gruber, H. E. 1974. *Darwin on Man: A Psychological Study of Scientific Creativity*. London: Wildwood House.

Hacking, I. 1968. One problem about induction. In *The Problem of Inductive Logic*, edited by I. Lakatos, 44–59. Cambridge: Cambridge University Press.

Haldane, J. B. S. 1932. *The Causes of Evolution*. New York: Cornell University Press.

Hall, S. E. 1997. The future of combinatorial chemistry as a drug discovery paradigm. *Pharmaceutical Research* 14: 1104–1112.

Hamburger, V. 1975. Cell death in the development of the lateral motor column of the chick embryo. *Journal of Comparative Neurology* 160: 535–546.

Hamilton, W. D. 1964. The genetical evolution of social behavior, I & II. *Journal of Theoretical Biology* 7: 1–52.

Hassan, F. A. 1981. *Demographic archaeology*. New York: Academic Press.

Haste, H. and J. Torney-Purta. 1992. *The Development of Political Understanding.* San Francisco: Jossey-Bass.

Hesse, M., and M. Arbib. 1986. *The Construction of Reality*. Cambridge: Cambridge University Press.

Holland, J. H. 1992. Genetic algorithms. *Scientific American* 267: 66–72.

Hook, J. and T. Cook. 1979. Equity theory and the cognitive ability of children. *Psychological Bulletin* 86: 429–445.

Hubbard, R. 1983. Have only men evolved? In *Discovering Reality*, edited by S. Harding, and M. B. Hintikka, 45–69. Dordrecht: Reidel.

Hull, D. L. 1978. Altruism in science: A sociobiological model of the cooperative behavior among scientists. *Animal Behavior* 26: 685–697.

———. 1982. The naked meme. In *Learning, Development and Culture: Essays in Evolutionary Epistemology*, edited by H. C. Plotkin. Chichester: Wiley.

———. 1986. Conceptual evolution and the eye of the octopus. In *Logic, Methodology and Philosophy of Science*, vol. 7, edited by R. B. Marcus, G. J. W. Dorn and P. Weingartner, 643–665. Amsterdam: North-Holland.

———. 1988a. *Science as a Process*. Chicago: University of Chicago Press.

———. 1988b. A mechanism and its metaphysics. *Biology & Philosophy* 3: 1–24.

———. 1999. The use and abuse of Sir Karl Popper. *Biology & Philosophy* 14: 481–504.

Humphrey, N. K. 1976. The social function of intellect. In *Growing Points in Ethology*, edited by P. P. G. Bateson and R. A. Hinde. Cambridge: Cambridge University Press.

Huttenlocher, P. R., and A. S. Dabholkar. 1997. Regional differences in synaptogenesis in human cerebral cortex. *Journal of Comparative Neurology* 367: 167–178.

Huxley, J. S. 1942. *Evolution: The Modern Synthesis*. London: Allen and Unwin.

———. 1959. Introduction to *The Phenomenon of Man*, by T. de Chardin, 11–28. London: Collins.

Jacobs, R. C. and D. T. Campbell. 1961. The perpetuation of an arbitrary tradition through several generations of a laboratory microculture. *Journal of Abnormal and Social Psychology* 62: 649–658.

James, W. 1907. *Pragmatism*. New York: Longmans, Green.

Jarvenpa, R., and H. Brumbach. 1988. Socio-spatial organization and decision-making processes: Observations from the Chipewyan. *American Anthropologist* 90: 598–618.

Jones, T. A., and T. Schallert. 1992. Overgrowth and pruning of dendrites in adult rats recovering from neocortical damage. *Brain Research* 581: 156–160.

———. 1994. Use-dependent growth of pyramidal neurons after neocortical damage. *Journal of Neuroscience* 14: 2140– 2152.

Joyce, G. F. 1992. Directed molecular evolution. *Scientific American* 267: 90–97.

Kantorovich, A. 1993. *Scientific Discovery: Logic and Tinkering*. Albany: State University of New York Press.

Keesing, R. M. 1974. Theories of culture. *Annual Review of Anthropology* 3: 73–97.

Kim, J. 1988. What is "Naturalized Epistemology"? *Philosophical Perspective*, vol. 2, Epistemology, 381–405.

Kim, K. M. 1994a. *Explaining Scientific Consensus: The Case of Mendelian Genetics*. New York: Guildford Press.

———. 1994b. Natural versus normative rationality: Reassessing the strong programme in the sociology of knowledge. *Social Studies of Science* 24: 391–403.

———. 1997. D. T. Campbell's social epistemology of science: Vicarious selection, epistemological fallibilism, and sociology of scientific validity. *Evolution and Cognition* 3: 75–80.

Kitcher, P. 1987. Confessions of a curmudgeon. *Behavioural and Brain Sciences* 10: 89–97.

Knorr-Cetina, K. 1981. *The Manufacture of Knowledge.* Oxford: Pergamon Press.

Köhler, W. 1925. *The Mentality of the Apes.* 2nd rev. ed., translated by E. Winter. New York: Harcourt, Brace.

Kornblith, H. 1985. *Naturalizing epistemology*. Cambridge, Mass.: MIT Press.

Koza, J. R. 1992. *Genetic Programming: On the Programming of Computers by Means of Natural Selection*. Cambridge, Mass.: MIT Press.

———. 1994. *Genetic Programming II: Automatic Discovery of Reusable Programs*. Cambridge, Mass.: MIT Press.

Kuhn, T. S. 1962. *The Structure of Scientific Revolutions*. Chicago: University of Chicago Press.

Kroeber, A. L. 1953. Concluding review. In *An Appraisal of Anthropology Today*, edited by S. Tax, L. C. Eisely, I. Rousse and C. F. Voegellin. Chicago: University of Chicago Press.

Kroeber, A. L., and C. Kluckholm. 1952. Culture: A critical review of the concepts and definitions. *Papers of the Peabody Museum of American Archaeology and Ethnology* 47: 1–22.

Kuper, A. 1999. *Culture: The Anthropologists' Account*. Cambridge, Mass.: Harvard University Press.

Lamarck, J. B. 1809. *Philosophie zoologique*. Paris: Dentu.

Latour, B. 1988. The politics of explanation: An alternative. In *Knowledge and Reflexivity*, edited by S. Woolgar. London: Sage.

Latour, B., and S. Woolgar. 1979. *Laboratory Life: The Construction of Scientific Facts.* Beverly Hills: Sage.

Lester, J. 1994. *E. Ray Lankester and the Making of Modern British Biology*, assisted by P. Bowler. Oxford: British Society for the History of Science Publications.

Lewontin, R. C. 1982. Organism and environment. In *Learning, Development, and Culture: Essays in Evolutionary Epistemology*, edited by H. C. Plotkin. Chichester: Wiley.

———. 1991. *Biology as Ideology: The Doctrine of DNA*. Toronto: Anansi.

Liang, D. W., R. Moreland, and L. Argote. 1995. Group versus individual training and group performance: The mediating role of transactive memory. *Personality And Social Psychology Bulletin* 21: 384–339.

Longino, H. 1990. *Science as Social Knowledge*. Princeton: Princeton University Press.

Lorenz, K. 1962. Kant's doctrine of a priori in the light of contemporary biology. *General Systems* 7: 23–35.

———. 1965. *The Evolution and Modification of Behaviour*. Chicago: University of Chicago Press.

Lumsden, C., and E. O. Wilson. 1981. *Genes, Mind and Culture*. Cambridge, Mass.: Harvard University Press.

Maynard Smith, J., and E. Szathmary. 1995. *The Major Transitions in Evolution*. New York: Oxford University Press.

Mayr, E. 1942. *Systematics and the Origin of Species*. New York: Columbia University Press.

———. 1982. *The Growth of Biological Thought*. Cambridge, Mass.: Harvard University Press.

———. 1988. *Towards a New Philosophy of Biology: Observations of an Evolutionist*. Cambridge, Mass.: Belknap.

McMullin, E. 1983. Values in science. *PSA 1982*, edited by P. D. Asquith and T. Nickles, 3–28. East Lansing: Philosophy of Science Association.

McNeill, M. 1987. *Under the Banner of Science: Erasmus Darwin and His Age*. Manchester: Manchester University Press.

Medawar, P. B. [1961] 1967. Review of *The Phenomenon of Man*, by T. de Chardin. *Mind* 70:99–106. In *The Art of the Soluble*, edited by P. Medawar. London: Methuen.

———. 1972. *The Hope of Progress*. London: Methuen.

Mednick, S. A. 1962. The associative basis of the creative process. *Psychological Review* 69: 220–232.

Moscovici, S. 1984. The phenomenon of social representations. In *Social Representations,* edited by R. M. Farr and S. Moscovici. Cambridge: Cambridge University Press.

Murdock, G. P. 1956. How culture changes. In *Man, Culture and Society*, edited by H. L. Shapiro. Oxford: Oxford University Press.

Nisbett, R., and L. Ross. 1980. *Human Inference: Strategies and Shortcomings of Social Judgment*. Englewood Cliffs, N.J.: Prentice-Hall.

Ospovat, D. 1981, reissue 1995. *The Development of Darwin's Theory: Natural History, Natural Theology, and Natural Selection, 1838–1859*. Cambridge: Cambridge University Press.

Outram, D. 1984. *Georges Cuvier: Vocation, Science and Authority in Post Revolutionary France*. Manchester: Manchester University Press.

Overman, E. S. 1988. *Methodology and epistemology for social science: Selected papers*. Chicago: University of Chicago Press.

Perutz, M. 1995. The pioneer defended. *New York Review of Books* 42(20): 54–58.

Pinch, T. 1986. Strata various. *Social Studies of Science* 16.

Pinker, S. 1994. *The Language Instinct.* London: Allen Lane.

———. 1997. *How the Mind Works*. New York: Norton.

Place, U. T. 2000. The role of the hand in the evolution of language. (vol. 11, no. 007) [on-line serial]. Available from ftp.princeton.edu/pub/harnad/psycoloquy/2000.volume.11/;INTERNET.

Plotkin, H.C. 1987. Evolutionary epistemology and the synthesis of biological and social science. In *Evolutionary Epistemology*, edited by W. Callebaut and R. Pinxten. Dordrecht: Reidel.

———. 1994. *Darwin Machines and the Nature of Knowledge*. Cambridge, Mass.: Harvard University Press.

———. 1996. Some psychological mechanisms of culture. *Philosophica* 57: 91–106.

———. 1997. *Evolution in Mind.* London: Allen Lane.

Plunkett, M. J., and J. A. Ellman. 1997. Combinatorial chemistry and new drugs. *Scientific American* 27: 68–73.

Popper, K. R. 1959. *The Logic of Scientific Discovery.* London: Hutchinson.

———. 1972. *Objective Knowledge.* Oxford: Oxford University Press.

Pringle, J. W. S. 1951. On the parallel between learning and evolution. *Behaviour* 3: 175–215.

Proctor, R. A. 1993. Computer stimulated associations. *Creativity Research Journal* 6: 391–400.

Pulliam, H. R., and C. Dunford. 1980. *Programmed to Learn: An Essay on the Evolution of Culture.* New York: Columbia University Press.

Quartz, S. R., and T. F. Sejnowski. 1997. The neural basis of cognitive development: A constructivist manifesto. *Behavioral and Brain Sciences* 20: 537–596.

Rainger, R. 1991. *An Agenda for Antiquity: Henry Fairfield Osborn and Vertebrate Paleontology at the American Museum of Natural History, 1890–1935.* Tuscaloosa: University of Alabama Press.

Restivo, S. 1997. In the wake of a winner: Donald T. Campbell and the sociology of objectivity. *Philosophica* 60: 57–73.

Reichenbach, H. 1949. *The Theory of Probability.* Berkeley: University of California Press.

Richards, R. J. 1981. Natural selection and other models in the historiography of science. In *Scientific Inquiry and the Social Sciences*, edited by M. B. Brewer and B. E. Collins, 37–76. San Francisco: Jossey-Bass.

———. 1987. *Darwin and the Emergence of Evolutionary Theories of Mind and Behavior.* Chicago: University of Chicago Press.

Rose, S. 1998. *Lifelines: Biology Beyond Determinism.* New York: Oxford University Press.

Rudwick, M. J. S. 1985. *The Great Devonian Controversy.* Chicago: University of Chicago Press.

Ruse, M. 1975. Darwin's debt to philosophy: An examination of the influence of the philosophical ideas of John F. W. Herschel and William Whewell on the development of Charles Darwin's theory of evolution. *Studies in History and Philosophy of Science* 6: 159–181.

———. 1979. *The Darwinian Revolution: Science Red in Tooth and Claw*. Chicago: University of Chicago Press.

———. 1983. Darwin and philosophy today. In *The Wider Domain of Evolutionary Thought,* edited by D. Oldroyd and I. Langham, 133–168. Dordrecht: D. Reidel.

———. 1986. *Taking Darwin Seriously: A Naturalistic Approach to Philosophy*. Oxford: Blackwell.

———. 1989. *The Darwinian Paradigm: Essays on its History, Philosophy and Religious Implications*. London: Routledge.

———. 1990. Does evolutionary epistemology imply realism? In *Evolution, Cognition and Realism,* edited by N. Rescher. Lanham, Md.: University Press of America.

———. 1993. Evolution and progress. *Trends in Ecology and Evolution* 8(2): 55–59.

———. 1996. *Monad to Man: The Concept of Progress in Evolutionary Biology*. Cambridge, Mass.: Harvard University Press.

———. 1999. *Mystery of Mysteries: Is Evolution a Social Construction*? Cambridge, Mass.: Harvard University Press.

Russell, B. 1948. *Human Knowledge*. New York: Simon & Schuster.

Schallert, T., and T. A. Jones. 1993. "Exuberant" neuronal growth after brain damage in adult rats: The essential role of behavioral experience. *Journal of Neurotransplantation and Plasticity* 4: 193–198.

Schilpp, P. A. 1974. *The Philosophy of Karl Popper*. LaSalle, Ill.: Open Court.

Searle, J. R. 1995. *The Construction of Social Reality*. London: Allen Lane.

Sevon, G., and S. Weckstrom. 1989. The development of reasoning about economic events. *Journal of Economic Psychology* 10: 495–514.

Shapin, S. 1979. The politics of observation: Cerebral anatomy and social interests in Edinburgh phrenology disputes. In *On the Margins of Science: The Social Construction of Rejected Knowledge,* edited by R. Wallace, Sociological Review Monograph 27: 39–87. Staffordshire, Eng.: Keele University.

Shapin, S., and S. Schaffer. 1985. *Leviathan and the Air-Pump: Hobbes, Boyle and the Experimental Life*. Princeton: Princeton University Press.

Sherif, M. 1935. A study of some social factors in perception. *Archives of Psychology* 27 (187): 1–60.

Shrader, D. 1979. The evolutionary development of science. *Review of Metaphysics* 34: 273–296.

Siegel, H. 1989. Philosophy of science naturalized? Some problems with Giere's naturalism. *Studies in History and Philosophy of Science* 20: 365–375.

Siegler, R. S. 1989. Mechanisms of cognitive development. *Annual Review of Psychology* 40: 353–379.

———. 1996. *Emerging Minds: The Process of Change in Children's Thinking*. New York: Oxford University Press.

Simonton, D. K. 1979. Multiple discovery and invention: Zeitgeist, genius, or chance? *Journal of Personality and Social Psychology* 37: 1603–1616.

———. 1985. Intelligence and personal influence in groups: Four nonlinear models. *Psychological Review* 92: 532–547.

———. 1987. Multiples, chance, genius, creativity, and zeitgeist. In *Scientific Excellence: Origins and Assessment*, edited by D. N. Jackson and J. P. Rushton. Beverly Hills: Sage.

———. 1997. Creative productivity: A predictive and explanatory model of career trajectories and landmarks. *Psychological Review* 104: 66–89.

———. 1999a. Creativity as blind variation and selective retention: Is the creative process Darwinian? *Psychological Inquiry* 10: 309–328.

———. 1999b. *Origins of Genius: Darwinian Perspectives on Creativity*. New York: Oxford University Press.

Simpson, G. G. 1944. *Tempo and Mode in Evolution*. New York: Columbia University Press.

———. 1949. *The Meaning of Evolution*. New Haven: Yale University Press.

Skagestad, P. 1978. Taking evolution seriously: Critical comments on D. T. Campbell's evolutionary epistemology. *Monist* 61: 611–621.

Smocovitis, V. B. 1992. Unifying biology: The evolutionary synthesis and evolutionary biology. *Journal of the History of Biology* 25: 1–66.

———. 1996. *Unifying Biology: The Evolutionary Synthesis and Evolutionary Biology*. Princeton: Princeton University Press.

Sober, E., and D. S. Wilson. 1998. *Unto Others: The Evolution and Psychology of Unselfish Behavior*. Cambridge, Mass.: Harvard University Press.

Song, M. J., J. G. Smetana, and S. Y. Kim. 1987. Korean childrens' conceptions of moral and conventional transgressions. *Developmental Psychology* 23: 577–582.

Spencer, H. 1852a. A theory of population, deduced from the general law of animal fertility. *Westminster Review* 1: 468–501.

———. [1852b] 1868. The development hypothesis. *The Leader*. Reprinted in H. Spencer, *Essays: Scientific, Political and Speculative*, 377–83. London: Williams and Norgate.

———. [1857] 1868. Progress: Its law and cause. *Westminster Review* 67: 244–267. Reprinted in H. Spencer, *Essays Scientific, Political and Speculative*. London: Williams and Norgate.

Stebbins, G. L. 1950. *Variation and Evolution in Plants*. New York: Columbia University Press.

———. 1969. *The Basis of Progressive Evolution*. Chapel Hill, N.C.: University of North Carolina Press.

Storer, N. W. 1973. *The Sociology of Science: Theoretical and Empirical Investigations*. Chicago: University of Chicago Press.

Szathmary, E., and J. Maynard Smith. 1995. The major evolutionary transitions. *Nature* 374: 227–232.

Thagard, P. 1988. *Computational Philosophy of Science*. Cambridge, Mass.: MIT Press.

———. 1994. Mind, society and the growth of knowledge. *Philosophy of Science* 61: 529–645.

Tobias, P. 1995. The communication of the dead: Earliest vestiges of the origin of articulate language talking with the dead. *Zeventiende Kroon-Voordracht.* Amsterdam: Stichting Nederlands Museum voor Anthropologie en Praehistorie.

Tomasello, M. 1999. *The Cultural Origins of Human Cognition.* Cambridge, Mass.: Harvard University Press.

Toulmin, S. 1967. The evolutionary development of natural science. *American Scientist* 55: 456–471.

———. 1972. *Human Understanding: The Evolution of Collective Understanding.* Princeton: Princeton University Press.

Vollmer, G. 1984. Mexocosm and objective knowledge. In *Concepts and Approaches in Evolutionary Epistemology,* edited by F. M. Wuketits, 69–121. Dordrecht: D. Reidel.

Vrba, E. S. 1986. The hierarchical expansion of sorting and selection: Sorting and selection cannot be equated. *Paleobiology* 12: 217–228.

Wagar, W. 1972. *Good Tidings: The Belief in Progress from Darwin to Marcuse.* Bloomington: Indiana University Press.

Weinberg, S. 1992. *Dreams of a Final Theory: The Search for the Fundamental Laws of Nature.* New York: Pantheon.

Whewell, W. 1840. *The Philosophy of the Inductive Sciences,* 2 vols. London: Parker.

Whiten, A., J. Goodall, W. C. McGrew, T. Nishida, V. Reynolds, Y. Sugiyama, C. E. G. Tutin, R. W. Wrangham, and C. Boesch. 1999. Culture in chimpanzees. *Nature* 399: 682–685.

Williams, G. C. 1966. *Adaptation and Natural Selection.* Princeton: Princeton University Press.

Wilson, D. S., and E. Sober. 1994. Reintroducing group selection to the human behavioural sciences. *Behavioural and Brain Sciences* 17: 585–608.

Wilson, E. O. 1975. *Sociobiology: The New Synthesis.* Cambridge, Mass.: Harvard University Press.

———. 1990. *Success and Dominance in Ecosystems: The Case of the Social Insects.* Oldendorf/Luhe: Ecology Institute.

———. 1992. *The Diversity of Life*. Cambridge, Mass.: Harvard University Press.

———. 1994. *Naturalist*. Washington, D.C.: Island Books/Shearwater Books.

Wimsatt, W. C. 1972. Teleology and the logical structure of function statement. *Studies in History and Philosophy of Science* 3: 1–80.

Woolgar, S. 1988. *Science: The Very Idea*. Chichester: Ellis Horwood.

Wright, S. [1931] 1986. Evolution in mendelian populations. *Genetics* 16: 2. In *Evolution: Selected Papers,* edited by W. B. Provine. Chicago: Chicago University Press.

———. [1932] 1986. The roles of mutation, inbreeding, crossbreeding and selection in evolution. In *Evolution: Selected Papers,* edited by W. B. Provine. Chicago: Chicago University Press.

Wuketits, F. M. 1990. *Evolutionary Epistemology and its Implications for Humankind.* Albany: State University of New York Press.

Young, R. M. 1985. *Darwin's Metaphor: Nature's Place in Victorian Culture.* Cambridge: Cambridge University Press.

Contributors

Michael Bradie is Professor of Philosophy at Bowling Green State University. He is author of *The Secret Chain: Evolution and Ethics* (1994) and has published papers on evolutionary ethics, evolutionary epistemology and the role of models and metaphors in science.

Linnda R. Caporael is a professor in the Department of Science and Technology Studies at Rensselaer Polytechnic Institute. She received her Ph.D. in psychology from the University of California, Santa Barbara. As a Fullbright-Hayes Scholar, she studied human ethology at the Institute of Child Development, University of London. Her interests include the evolution of human sociality; group coordination; social identity; the attribution of human characteristics to animals, machines, and artificial agents; and the design of culturally "fit" artifacts. Her work has appeared in *Science, Journal of Personality and Social Psychology, Behavioral and Brain Sciences*, and other journals and books.

Gary A. Cziko is Professor of Educational Psychology at the University of Illinois at Urbana-Champaign. Among his interests are the applications of biological principles originating with Charles Darwin and Claude Bernard to psychology and education. His two books in this vein are *Without*

Miracles (1995) and *The Things We Do* (2000), both published by MIT Press. He has also conducted research on first and second language acquisition.

Ronald N. Giere is Professor of Philosophy and a former Director of the Center for Philosophy of Science at the University of Minnesota. In addition to many papers in the philosophy of science, he is the author of *Understanding Scientific Reasoning* (4th ed. 1997); *Explaining Science: A Cognitive Approach* (1988); and *Science Without Laws* (1999). He has also edited several volumes of papers in the philosophy of science, including, most recently, *Cognitive Models of Science* (1992) and *Origins of Logical Empiricism* (1996). Prof Giere is a Fellow of The American Association for the Advancement of Science, a long-time member of the editorial board of the journal *Philosophy of Science*, and a Past President of the Philosophy of Science Association.

Cecilia Heyes is a professor in Psychology at University College London. After her Ph.D., she studied evolutionary epistemology for two years (1984–86) with Donald Campbell as a Harkness Fellow of the Commonwealth Fund of New York. Subsequently, as a Research Fellow of Trinity Hall, University of Cambridge (1986-89) and at University College London, her experimental work has focused on psychological mechanisms of social learning in animals, and her theoretical work on the evolution of intentional representation. Her research has been published in *Advances in the Study of Behavior, Animal Behaviour, Behavioral and Brain Sciences, Biological Reviews, Biology and Philosophy*, *Journal of Comparative Psychology*, *Learning and Motivation*, and *Mind and Language*. She has recently co-edited (with Ludwig Huber) a book, *The Evolution of Cognition*.

David L. Hull is professor emeritus in the Department of Philosophy, Northwestern University, Evanston, Illinois. He has published over a hundred articles and five books, including *Science as a Process* (1988) and *Science and Selection* (2000). He works in the philosophy of biology, primarily evolutionary biology and classification, as well as philosophy of science more generally.

Kyung-Man Kim is professor of sociology at Sogang University, Seoul, Korea. He is author of *Explaining Scientific Consensus: The Case of Mendelian Genetics* (Guildford Press 1994). His research interests include sociology of science and social theory. Recently, he has published articles in *The Sociological Quarterly*, *The American Sociologist*, and *Philosophy of the Social Sciences*.

Henry Plotkin was born and raised in South Africa. He came to England in the 1960s and was graduated with a Ph.D. from the University of London in 1968. He did a spell as a postdoctoral student on a Medical Research Council Fellowship at Stanford University and worked for both the Medical Research Council and University College London. He was chair of the Department of Psychology for the period 1993-1998 and currently is Science Director of the ESRC Research Centre on Economic Learning and Social Evolution. He has published two books, *Darwin Machines and the Nature of Knowledge* (1993) and *Evolution in Mind* (1998), both published by Penguin in the UK and Harvard University Press in the United States. He has edited and co-edited three anthologies and published around a hundred journal papers, book chapters, etc. In 1993 he was awarded a personal Chair in Psychology at University College London.

Michael Ruse is Lucyle T. Werkmeister Professor at Florida State University in Tallahassee, Florida. He has published over a dozen books, including *The Philosophy of Biology* (1973), *The Darwinian Revolution* (1979), *Sociobiology: Sense or Nonsense?* (1985), *Monad to Man* (1996), *Taking Darwin Seriously* (1998), and *Mystery of Mysteries* (1999). He is also founder and editor of the journal *Biology and Philosophy*, editor of the Cambridge Series in the Philosophy of Biology, and on the editorial boards of many other journals.

Index